Globalization and
Its Enemies

Globalization and Its Enemies

Daniel Cohen

translated by
Jessica B. Baker

The MIT Press
Cambridge, Massachusetts
London, England

First MIT Press paperback edition, 2007

© 2006 Massachusetts Institute of Technology
(*La Mondialisation et ses ennemis* © Editions Grasset & Fasquelle, 2004)

MIT Press books may be purchased at special quantity discounts for business or sales promotional use. For information, please email special_sales@mitpress.mit.edu or write to Special Sales Department, The MIT Press, 55 Hayward Street, Cambridge, MA 02142.

Set in Palatino by SNP Best-set Typesetter Ltd., Hong Kong. Printed and bound in the United States of America.

Library of Congress Cataloging-in-Publication Data

Cohen, Daniel, 1953–.
[Mondialisation et ses ennemis. English]
Globalization and its enemies / Daniel Cohen ; translated by Jessica B. Baker.
    p. cm.
Includes bibliographical references and index.
ISBN-13: 978-0-262-03350-3 (hc.: alk. paper)—978-0-262-53297-6 (pb.: alk. paper)
ISBN-10: 0-262-03350-X (hc.: alk. paper)—0-262-53297-2 (pb.: alk. paper)
1. Globalization—Economic aspects. 2. Globalization. I. Title
HF1359.C64813   2006
303.48′2—dc22   2006041996

10 9 8 7 6 5

Contents

in memory of my father

Acknowledgments

I thank Michel Cohen, Olivier Mongin, Pierre Rosanvallon, and Perrine Simon-Nahum for their valuable help with the manuscript, and the students at Ecole normale supérieure who participated in the seminars "From One Globalization, the Other" and "The Post-Industrial Economy" for the stimulation they provided.

Globalization and
Its Enemies

Introduction

Why are poor countries so poor and rich countries so rich? The simple response attributes the disparity to exploitation of the former by the latter. History compares the position of poor countries today to that of slaves in antiquity or that of the working class in industrialized countries. Though there may be some merit to this comparison, the intuition behind it is radically false. Exploitation has not caused the suffering of poor countries. It would be better to say that these countries suffer from having been abandoned to their fate. The poorest countries are not like the workers at the center of industrial capitalism; their situation is closer to that of individuals lost in the French welfare system today. "The West did not need the Third World," the economic historian Paul Bairoch concluded.[1] That, I would add, was bad news for the Third World. To say that the West depends little or not at all on Africa does not exonerate it of blame for the misery found in the Third World, but the relationship between the West and the Third World is not that of exploiter and exploited.

To understand the nature of this complicated relationship, let us consider the surprise of Germaine Tillion, a French anthropologist who had lived in a mountain village in the Aurès region of Algeria in the 1930s, when she returned to the region 20 years later.[2] The Aurès society that Germaine Tillion first knew, a society that she perceived as "balanced and happy in its ancestral tranquility," had become impoverished. What had been the cause? "Nothing or scarcely anything." Believing they were helping Aurès by bringing civilization, the French dispersed DDT in the ponds to combat malaria and typhoid fever and built a road to end the region's isolation. Then they went home. These two innovations produced a chain reaction. The eradication of typhoid and malaria triggered a demographic explosion. In one generation, the population doubled. To meet the needs that resulted from this increase, shepherds had to enlarge their herds. The livestock rapidly destroyed the soil. Thanks to the road, some people were able to export their surplus livestock. Some became rich; others fell into debt; some were ruined. The inequality became apparent. The richest members of this society sent their children to the school in the nearest large town. The Koranic tradition was quickly devalued.

Like a population destroyed by an epidemic, "the traditional society disintegrated by this slight contact, this slight brush with Western civilization." There was no exploitation. This example poses questions that transcend the simple categories of Good and Evil. When we build a road between a mountainous region and a city, thus relieving the isolation that bears some responsibility for the mountainous region's poverty, are we putting into motion forces that will conflict with ancestral authority and increase inequality? Will we come to regret that isolation no longer remains the norm? Still more complicated is the fact that by fighting malaria in Aurès the French unleashed a population explosion. Should we let children die for fear of unsettling the demographic equilibrium of ancestral life? Does a reduction in child mortality, which seems to be one of the benefits conferred by modern society, impart with it the entire model of industrial society? Must it be irremediably inscribed as a unique diagram, associated in the West with a "demographic transition," whereby reducing infant mortality entails a decline in fertility, a change which is inevitably accompanied by education of children, liberation of women from the patriarchal order, and (finally) entry into "modern" life? These complex questions cannot be answered either Yes or No. They are questions that come from afar.

The present globalization is just the third act in a story that began half a millennium ago. The first act began with the discovery of America in the sixteenth century, the age of the Spanish Conquistadors. The second act was the nineteenth century, the age of the English merchants. The first globalization began a sequence very similar to the tragedy described by Germaine Tillion. It was not medicine that the Spanish Conquistadors brought with them, but rather smallpox, measles, influenza, and typhoid. The process is, however, the same. One civilization destroys the other, not because it is more "advanced," but because it is immune to its own diseases, protected against the perverse effects of its system. Today, as yesterday, a considerable number of poor countries are destroyed by the fact that they are not protected against the perverse effects of industrial society and of urbanization, or against the lifestyle they entail.

In the nineteenth century, Great Britain, a grand empire adept at free trade, dominated the world thanks to a revolution in transportation and communication brought on by the railroad, the steamship, and the telegraph. If there is a lesson to learn from the nineteenth century, it is that reducing the costs of transportation and communication is not sufficient to spread prosperity. India was just as poor in 1913 as it was in 1820, despite a century as a member of the Commonwealth. The paradox that economists have been late to understand is that reducing the costs of transportation and communication does not promote wealth but instead favors its polarization. With the railroad, small market villages and hamlets disappear because they cannot survive the competition from big towns and cities. When a railroad connects two towns, it is the larger of the two that will prosper, and in most cases the smaller one disappears. This is the exact phenomenon that the French unleashed when they built a road to break the isolation of Aurès. Likewise, today's information economy and today's modes of communication favor the major players and do not give new entrants a chance. Far from delivering the free entry and the transparency dreamed of by economists, the so-called information society creates its own barriers, replacing those that technology breaks down.

The enemies of globalization are arrayed in two opposed camps, each drawing support from this testimony of History. One camp, to simplify, is that of the Mullahs who denounce the "Westernization of the world." The other camp is that of the enemies of capitalism, who fight the exploitation of workers by capital. The first camp fights the war between civilizations, the second the global class struggle. Despite their differences, these two opposing camps find themselves clinging to the idea that globalization imposes a model that people do not want. The truth, however, is probably the reverse. Globalization shows people a world that subverts their expectations; the drama lies in the fact that this revelation is incapable of satisfying them. When we are moved by televised images of poor children, we forget that these same children (or their parents) are also watching us on television, which for them is a window on our material prosperity. It is, above all, roads and medicines that poor countries demand, at the moment that their gaze crosses ours. To understand the current act of globalization within the confines of religion or exploitation is to miss globalization's singularity.

Today's globalization is radically different from its predecessors on one essential point: It is difficult to be an actor but easy to be a spectator. Films get more and more expensive to produce, and medical research more and more complex. However, a movie can be shown just as easily in the suburbs of Cairo as in those of Los Angeles, and medicine heals the poor and the rich. The new global economy creates an unprecedented rupture between the expectations to which it gives birth and the reality it brings about. Never before have means of communication—the media—created such a global consciousness; never have the economic forces been so far behind this new awareness. For the majority of the poor inhabitants of our planet, globalization is only a fleeting image. What we too often ignore, however, is how strong this image is, how pregnant with promises yet to be fulfilled.

Nothing better illustrates the new closeness between the rich and the poor than the demographic transition. A population explosion occurred in Aurès as a result of decreased child mortality. However, in an unforeseen way, demographic transition is advancing today in a large majority of poor countries. The most important phenomenon in human history is, curiously, the most unrecognized, except among specialists. Everywhere in the world, whatever the religion—in Egypt, in Indonesia,

in China, in India, in Brazil, in Mexico, and elsewhere—
women are upsetting the traditional model. The number
of children born is falling at a rate of nearly one per
woman per decade, according to the United Nations. This
decline in the birth rate owes little to economic forces. It
can be observed in the cities as well as in the country,
whether women work or not. It is attributable to the
diffusion of a "cultural" model. Young Chinese women
want to imitate young Japanese women, who envy the
freedom of young American women and adopt their
habits. The diffusion of this model does not mean that
women in the Third World are culturally brutalized by
the Western media. It is fairer to acknowledge adherence
to a model which women around the world have seized
upon because they find in it an idea of freedom. The
enthusiasm that was aroused in Iranian women when
Shirine Ebadi was awarded the Nobel Peace Prize speaks
for itself. The reputedly impenetrable barriers between
civilizations are shown to be, in reality, quite porous.

To understand today's globalization requires that one
renounce the idea that the poor are stunted or exploited
by globalization. When India and China joined the World
Trade Organization, it was not out of naiveté or fear of
the great industrial powers; their firm attitude toward the
rich countries at the Cancun summit in September 2003
showed that. They had no illusion about the spontaneous
propensity of the capitalist world to diffuse its wealth.
But if the history of the nineteenth century taught them

that trade itself was not a factor in economic growth, the twentieth century showed them that protectionism was an even worse solution. Today everyone is searching for a new way.

Each in its own way, all countries are looking to bridge the divide that exists between the world's expectations and its realities. Of course this should not prevent us from critically examining globalization or from being concerned about the threats it presents to the planet's ecological and cultural equilibrium. But the main mistake to avoid is considering as an accomplished fact something that remains to occur for the majority of the world's population. It is because of what has yet to happen, and not what has already taken place, that globalization is a source of frustration to many. To be mistaken on this point is to build a critique of our world on a brittle foundation.

1

The Birth of the North-South Axis

The Conquest of the World

The scene is in 1532 in Cajamarca, a town on the upper Peruvian plateau. Leading 168 men, Francisco Pizarro faces the Incan emperor, Atahualpa. The absolute monarch of the most vast and most advanced New World empire heads an army of 80,000 soldiers. Pizarro captures Atahualpa, demands and receives a ransom, then kills him. The fight between Pizarro's forces and the troops of the murdered emperor begins. Against all numerical logic and on unfamiliar turf, the Spanish prevail. How was this possible? In *Guns, Germs, and Steel: The Fates of Human Societies,*[1] Jared Diamond stakes out a theory that may constitute the basis of what might be called "ecological materialism." It may also explain the origin, if not the persistence, of the inequalities between nations.

Pizarro and his men had swords, steel armor, muskets, and horses, while Atahualpa's troops had only cudgels, clubs, axes, and catapults made of stone, bronze, and wood. They had no firearms. A second factor is that the Spanish made use of written communication while the Incas did not. Atahualpa was poorly informed about the Spanish. When Pizarro disembarked on the Peruvian coast, the Incas did not know that Panama, just 960 kilometers to the north, had been conquered 16 years earlier. Pizarro, though illiterate himself, had profited from information that had allowed Cortes to seize the Aztec emperor, Montezuma. As with the Aztecs, the Incan empire was founded on a totally centralized political organization. By capturing and killing Atahualpa, Pizarro destroyed the Incas' chain of command. One last point: The Incas had no animals to use in battle against Pizarro's horses. It is a direct disadvantage but one that contains a weakness infinitely more important: the absence of resistance to infectious diseases. The main lethal agents that affect humanity—smallpox, flu, tuberculosis, malaria, plague, measles, and cholera—are all infectious diseases derived from animal illnesses, even though today these sicknesses no longer affect animals. Throughout history, individual carriers of resistant genes have had better chances of survival. Populations repeatedly exposed to pathogenic agents were in the end saved by this contact. On the eve of the battle against Pizarro, a smallpox epidemic decimated the Incas. Smallpox, measles, influenza. and typhus alone eliminated 95 percent of the indigenous pre-Columbian population.

Yali's Question

When the sixteenth century's overseas conquests forced encounters between civilizations, there was a sharp contrast between their levels of technical development. Eurasia (that is, Europe, Asia, and North Africa) was composed of empires or states, some on the verge of industrialization and familiar with metallurgy. At the same time, the Aztecs and the Incas ruled over their empires with stone implements. Sub-Saharan Africa was composed of small states and chiefdoms. Other peoples, in Australia, in New Guinea, on numerous Pacific islands, and in certain parts of sub-Saharan Africa, lived as agricultural tribes and sometimes hunter-gatherer groups who also used stone utensils.

"Why is it that you white people developed so much cargo and brought it to New Guinea, but we black people had little cargo of our own?"[2] A man named Yali posed this question to Jared Diamond, an American biologist who had gone to study the evolution of birds in New Guinea. Two centuries earlier, white men had arrived there, imposing a government on a population that lived in villages and bringing with them goods whose value the New Guineans recognized: metal axes, candles, medicine, non-alcoholic drinks, parasols. The New Guineans called these various goods "cargo." Yali's question continued to haunt Diamond. "I didn't have an answer then," he explained. "Professional historians still disagree about the solution; most are no longer even asking the question."[3] Twenty-five years later, Diamond set out to find an answer. "Why did wealth and power become distributed as they now are, rather than in some other way? For instance, why weren't Native Americans, Africans, and Aboriginal Australians the ones who decimated, subjugated, or exterminated the Europeans and the Asians?"[4] The answer to these questions shapes one's idea of globalization, if one is willing to admit that today's globalization prolongs the obstinate history of the human adventure.[5]

False Answers

The racist argument for the supposed superiority of the white race is brilliantly deconstructed by Diamond. Speaking soberly in the first person, he says: "My perspective on this controversy comes from 33 years of working with New Guineans in their own intact societies. From the very beginning of my work with New Guineans, they impressed me as being on the average more intelligent, more alert, more expressive, and more interested in things and people around them than the average European or American is."[6] Diamond suggests two explanations. The first, inspired by Neo-Darwinism, is that in the traditional New Guinean society the most intelligent individuals had a better chance than the rest to escape the causes of mortality, such as murder, tribal warfare, or simply the difficulty of procuring food. The second explanation holds that if a child's development

depends on stimulation and activity during early childhood, then the childhood of a young aborigine is certainly more stimulating that that of a Western child. In an
American living room, the television stays on 7 hours a
day. "In contrast, traditional New Guinea children have
virtually no such opportunities for passive entertain-
ment and instead spend nearly all of their waking hours
actively doing something, such as talking or playing with
other children or adults."[7] Diamond emphasizes that
each time a technologically primitive people is given the
means to use an industrial technique that may be
useful to them, they have no difficulty quickly instituting
it.[8]

A second response to the question of unequal economic development, already largely acknowledged,
would have to do with climate. Perhaps the long winters
that required people to stay indoors made them more apt
to think. Such is the case if one believes Pascal. But it is
easy to refute this answer. People from Northern Europe
(where it is cold) hardly made any fundamental contribution to civilization before the last millennium. The four
fundamental components of economic development—
agriculture, the wheel, writing, and metallurgy—were
all discovered in the warmest parts of Eurasia. This
same assertion holds in the New World, where the
only American societies that invented writing were in
Mexico or south of the Tropic of Cancer, and the society
generally considered most advanced in the arts and in

astronomy was the classic Mayan society, located in the Yucatan and in Guatemala.

The Answer to Yali

How, then, can we make sense of the inequalities between civilizations? Diamond's thesis is clear and probing. The variation between continents has nothing to do with climate or genetics. It is all due to the presence of animals that can be domesticated and plants that can be cultivated. Certain human communities lived in regions where sustained agriculture was possible, and others did not.[9] The vast majority of wild plants do not lend themselves to cultivation. The essential part of the biomass consists of indigestible wood and leaves. In the modern world, ten plant species represent more than 80 percent of annual cultivated crops: wheat, corn, rice, barley, sorghum, soybeans, potatoes, cassava, sweet potatoes, and bananas.

The Fertile Crescent of the Near East, at the origin of the entire chain of development that produced cities, writing, and then empires, is, above all, a region where cereal cultivation is simply very productive. In New Guinea, at the other end of the chain, food production quickly found itself restrained by the absence of domesticable cereal crops and animals. As shown by the enthusiastic adoption of the sweet potato, the inhabitants of these regions are perfectly capable of recognizing useful additions to their diet. In North America, the indigenous peoples had not wholly neglected the potentially useful cultivations of wild species, but "even twentieth-century plant breeders, armed with all the power of modern science, have had little success in exploiting North American wild plants."

Animals provide another striking example of Diamond's idea about what fosters economic growth. If we count all the "large" mammals (those that weigh more than 100 pounds), on the entire planet we find that only 14 species were domesticated before the twentieth century, nine of which were "minor" (that is, found in a radius of limited diffusion) and only five of which were properly capable of being universally exported. The five species that have been distributed around the world are the cow, the sheep, the goat, the pig, and the horse.[10] The history of the horse, which to past civilizations was what the railroad was to industrial societies, perfectly corroborates this theory. The horse was domesticated on the steppes north of the Black Sea around 4000 B.C. It was present only in Eurasia; the first Americans never saw it. However, it only required a single generation of indigenous North and South Americans to adopt the horse, by capturing animals that escaped from the European settlements. The horse was the principle agent of expansion, beginning with the Ukraine, of Indo-European-speaking populations. When horses were harnessed to combat chariots, around 1800 B.C., this revolutionized the art of war in the Near East.[11] In West Africa, the arrival of the domesticated horse transformed the region into an ensemble of tributary kingdoms of cavalries. If they did not expand beyond this point, it is because trypanosome transmitted by the tsetse fly prevented it. Zebras, so close in appearance to the horse, absolutely do not lend themselves to domestication. They have a naturally skittish character and a tendency to bite, and they become very badly behaved as they get old.[12]

The North-South Axis

The majority of agricultural innovations that came from the Fertile Crescent were propagated in the south up to the cool mountains of Ethiopia. Then the dissemination stopped. The quasi-Mediterranean climate of South Africa, however, would have been perfectly suited to plants typically cultivated in the Near East. But to be further diffused, they would have had to overcome the considerable obstacle that is the Sahara Desert. South of the Sahara, the cultivated plants have thus remained the local ones: sorghum and African yams. The southward movement of domesticated animals was slowed or prevented for the same reason. The progression of cattle, sheep, and goats also stalled at the edge of the northern plains of the Serengeti for nearly 2,000 years. The same holds true for the axis between North and South America. The distance between Central America and South America does not exceed 1,180 miles, about the distance that separates Mesopotamia from the Balkans. Never-theless, the Balkans, offering ideal climatic conditions, adopted all the domestic Mesopotamian species in less than 2,000 years. Similarly, Mexico's high and fresh land was perfectly suited for raising llamas and guinea pigs and cultivating potatoes—all present in the cool Andean climate in South America. Yet the northern progression of the potato and these animals was stopped by the hot plains of Central America. Five thousand years after the domestication of the llama in the Andes, Mexico's indigenous peoples had no edible mammal except the dog.

One natural dimension explains the difference between Eurasia and the other continents. Eurasia stretches along an East-West axis, while the Americas and Africa follow a North-South axis. Eurasia's regions share the same seasonal variations. The dispersal of agricultural innova-tions consequently occurs much faster. Southern Italy, Iran, and Japan are about 3,900 miles apart, but, since they are on the same latitude, their agriculture possesses common climactic characteristics. During the time of Christ, cereals originating in the Fertile Crescent grew on a 10,000-mile expanse ranging from Ireland to Japan! Soon after its discovery around 8000 B.C., agriculture propagation took place in Greece, Cyprus, and the Indian sub-continent by 6500 B.C., in Egypt around 6000 B.C., in meridian Spain by 5200 B.C., and in England by 3500 B.C. This crop cultivation was followed by other innovations originating in the Fertile Crescent: the wheel, writing, metallurgy, fruit trees, beer, wine.

Diamond anticipated the questions that one cannot help but raise: Is human history, then, only a mechanical development of ecological endowments? Are human beings merely passive robots without resources, programmed by climate, fauna, and flora? Is globalization limited to an unforeseen manifestation of natural phenomena? Diamond responds: "Of course these fears are misplaced. Without human inventiveness, all of us today would still be cutting our meat with stone tools and eating it raw, like our ancestors of a million years ago. It's just that some environments provide more starting materials, and more favorable conditions for utilizing inventions, than do other environments."[13] In fact, Diamond presses his conceptual advantage even further. He notes that a fair number of fundamental discoveries were invented only once. Thus is the case for "the water wheel, rotary quern, tooth gearing, magnetic compass, windmill, and camera obscura."[14] The most ingenious invention by far is the alphabet, even though it appeared only a single time in the entire human history! It comes to us from the speakers of Semitic languages living in the region between modern Syria and the Sinai, about 3,000 years ago. The hundreds of alphabets that once existed or that still exist today are derived from this ancestral Semitic alphabet. In demonstrating that the most important inventions are rare, even unique, Diamond suggests that, in the discoveries of the mind, chance plays at least as important a role as ecological happenstance. The alphabet was not "necessary" for agricultural societies, certainly no more than the horse: human genius, in all that is unforeseen, is singular in cause.

The Tyranny of Others

A simple lesson of Diamond's fascinating work is that "globalization" has always been a part of human history. Cultural diversity, resulting from ecological chance or the human spirit, is irrepressible, and it originates the inter-mingling of civilizations. Only the oceans and the deserts posed enduring obstacles to this headstrong march. In a 1993 article in the *Quarterly Journal of Economics*, Michael Kremer noted that at the time of the greatest discoveries of the sixteenth century the largest territories were more densely populated than the smallest ones.[15] Eurasia had more inhabitants per square mile than America, which had more than Australia, which had more than Tasmania, and so on. The theories just set forth help us to understand why. Vast territories have ecological variety, which allows them to create an autocatalytic process: more population, more inventions, more popu-lation. . . . From this process Kremer posited an encour-aging trend: The bigger the territory (today one would say "the bigger the market"), the more likely that this autocatalytic phenomenon (which economists call "endogenous growth") will happen.

Nothing within this argument, however, indicates a victory of good over evil. "Advanced" societies are not "happier" than those they ousted. Life in China is not a happier existence than life in Tahiti. Tahiti practiced infanticide at a high rate, whereas the Chinese found ways to feed an abundant population. This difference does not establish the superiority of the second model over the first, but it does make the second civilization indisputably more threatening than the first. It is less often by persuasion than by destruction that agricultural societies replace the hunter-gatherer groups they encounter. When an innovation like the domestication of the horse or the invention of writing comes along, either it is adopted by the society it confronts or it is rapidly destroyed by the societies that seize it. One learns from Diamond still another lesson of how "wealth" is diffused. The density of "advanced" societies allows them to develop antibodies to viruses that they themselves created and which decimate others. The more complex a society, the more it destroys less advanced societies in its path, having "immunized" its own members against the perverse effects of the technical system it produced. The Aurès tragedy cannot be explained in any other way. The French colonizers, even if they believed they were helping, brought answers to questions that no one was asking. In doing so, they also created problems to which these responses were destined. This assessment does not underestimate the revolutionary impact of rice, wheat, the horse, or the alphabet. It is astonishing to learn that American Indians, whom one cannot picture other than on horseback, only discovered the horse thanks to Christopher Columbus. That the Native Americans succumbed not to the civilization that brought the horse but to the illnesses people of that civilization transmitted is extraordinary.

A first lesson may be drawn: since the beginning, all human societies have been subject to what can be called "the tyranny of others." In another context, Claude Lévi-Strauss shows how myths are often a common type, corresponding to nostalgia for a golden age that is slipping away or waiting for the arrival of a messianic age. "At either end of the earth and at both extremes of time, the Sumerian myth of the golden age and the Andaman myth of the future life correspond . . . i.e., removing to an equally unattainable past or future the joys, eternally denied to social man, of a world in which one might *keep to oneself.*"[16] It is this world "to oneself" that has been denied humans since the beginning of time.

The relevance of these questions to those posed by "our" globalization seems obvious. Societies less advanced than ours certainly are not immune to the perverse effects of our technological world. Capitalism, for many, would not be particularly at fault. In the particular terms it lays down, is not this the path of ongoing human history? This complex and passionate question is not, however, the most important question to pose. The central issue regarding globalization is not that it develops too quickly or that its effects are too brutal. On the relatively short time scale of capitalism, what is striking is its poor capacity to diffuse technical progress rather than its propensity to impose progress everywhere.

2 From One Globalization to Another

Nothing is more favorable to the diffusion of knowledge and technology than a world where distances are obliterated, or where everyone could communicate with whomever they want without difficulty. The validity of this idea, which seems to characterize our current globalization, has already been partially refuted in the history books. The communication revolution, presented today as the great innovation of the twenty-first century, in effect happened once already in the nineteenth century. During that period, the telegraph, the railroad, and the telephone disrupted distances much more radically than the Internet does today. During the age of the Roman Empire, the average time for information to go from Rome to Alexandria was one hour per two-thirds of a mile. In the eighteenth century, it still took four days to send a letter from London to a recipient 186 miles away. Starting in 1865, London and Bombay were connected by cables laid underwater and across land. Information then took 24 hours to be transmitted from one end of the chain to the other. At the end of the nineteenth century, Bombay, Calcutta, Madras, Shanghai, and Hong Kong were connected to London at a cost not substantially higher than that of sending a message from London to Edinburgh. If the era of the Spanish Conquistadors marked the first act in modern globalization, then the second one took place in the nineteenth century at the English merchant houses.

The first regular transatlantic shipping route was inaugurated in 1838. In 1871, a fundamental innovation, the refrigerator, allowed the United States and Argentina to export frozen beef to Europe. In 1876, New Zealand began exporting butter. The Suez Canal opened on November 17, 1869, halving the shipping distance between London and Bombay. The integration of financial markets with markets in raw materials was nearly perfect. Kevin O'Rourke and Jeffrey Williamson calculated that in 1870 the price of wheat was 57 percent higher in Liverpool than in Chicago, but that in 1913 the difference was not more than 15 percent.[1] Similarly, in 1870 the price of cotton was 60 percent higher in Liverpool than in Bombay. The difference fell to less than 20 percent by 1913. In 1870 the price of rice in London was twice that in Rangoon; by 1913 the spread was no more than 20 percent. Regarding interest rates and financial mobility, the overall results are just as spectacular. "What an extraordinary episode in the economic progress of man

that age was which came to an end in August 1914! . . .
The inhabitant of London could order by telephone,
sipping his morning tea in bed, the varieties of products
of the whole earth. . . ."[2] Written by John Maynard Keynes
just after World War I, this passage illustrates the enthusiasm for a world of new dimensions. But it is the opinion
of an Englishman. The southern version of this story is
very different. In effect, there are two divergent histories
of the nineteenth century. To simplify, one is that of the
London resident who places orders by telephone, and the
other of the people to whom the orders are addressed.
Two completely different axes of globalization take
shape. One is a north-north axis principally sustained by
the mobility of people and favorable to a convergence of
living standards. The other is a north-south axis defined
by commerce in merchandise that accelerates the divergence of destinies.

America, America

The first axis was opened by the considerable mass
migration populating new territories which would
become countries (including the United States, Canada,
Argentina, and Australia). In his beautiful film *America,
America*, Elia Kazan recounts the suffering his uncle
endured in leaving his Turkish village to come to New
York, where, by working as a shoe shiner, he could eventually send for his family.[3] By railroad or by steamship,

millions of people crossed the world. Chinese traversed Asia and reached California. Indians embarked for Africa and the Caribbean. Sweden, Ireland, Southern Italy, and Eastern Europe sent masses of immigrants to the United States. Nearly 60 million Europeans left the overpopulated Old Continent for the abundant lands of the New World. No other migration in history compares to that of the nineteenth century, with the exception of the forced migration of some 8 million African slaves to the Americas and the Caribbean.[4]

This movement of people, the hallmark of the nineteenth century, began with a rural exodus. Like a tooth uprooted from the jaw, the human species brutally broke off—over the course of several decades in the extreme case of England, more slowly over a century for other industrialized countries—the 10,000 years of sedentary way of life in place since the invention of agriculture. The ancient world was rich in people and poor in land. In the New World, the situation was the exact reverse. The influence of these migrations was considerable, both for the sending countries and for the host countries. The price of land collapsed in Europe and exploded in the newly settled lands, while wages followed a rigorously inverse movement.[5] According to O'Rourke and Williamson, this migratory movement essentially explains why the income difference between England (Europe's richest country) and such peripheral European countries as Ireland and Sweden narrowed during that period.

Although it may be tempting to draw a parallel between today's globalization and that of the nineteenth century, there is a fundamental difference that makes such a comparison rather perilous. Today's globalization is "immobile." Merchandise is traded among all parts of the world, but it is only through television, or during a few vacation weeks for tourists from rich countries, that one encounters other societies. Yesterday's globalization was very different, at least in regard to Europeans populating new lands. The effects of this globalization were not achieved through commodities or images but principally through people who physically—not "virtually"— left one world for another. In 1913, immigrants made up about 10 percent of the world's population. Today it is 3 percent.

In the wake of human mobility came the movement of property. The order of magnitude is again disproportionate in relation to the current capital movements. If it is measured, for example, by the fraction of British savings invested abroad, the result is an amount that is stunning by today's standards. On the eve of World War I, about 50 percent of England's savings were invested overseas. At the same time, France exported 25 percent of its savings. For the most part English capital flowed to, in this order, Canada, Australia, New Zealand, and the

United States. India, the Commonwealth's most populated country, received only a meager portion of English
capital.[6] The nature of these foreign investments is in
tandem with the migratory movements. Effectively,
English investments financed major infrastructures,
notably the new railroad lines, which the lands of
emigration needed to absorb European manpower.
For theoreticians of this period (e.g. Rosa Luxemburg),
the exportation of capital seemed to be one of the
conditions of capitalism's existence. According to some
contemporary historians, London's attracting foreign
investment deprived England of the fruits of its
savings. In every hypothesis, the comparison with the
current situation is astonishing. The flow of capital
and workers is much more limited today. This prompts
some economists to say that today's globalization,
in reality, is much smaller than the nineteenth-century
one.

The International Division of Labor

What renders the nineteenth-century globalization so
worrisome in the eyes of those who have analyzed it is
that it permitted Europe to pursue its work of making the
rest of the planet subservient. At the heart of the current
debate on the effects of globalization is the question of
why the great Eurasian civilizations of the past—Islam,
India, China—lost so much ground relative to Europe,

whereas North America and Australia, though far from the "center," experienced sharp growth.

During the entire first half of the nineteenth century, India was privately managed by the East India Company, an uncommon experience in the history of civilizations. Among economists who attribute the Third World's problems to bad "governance," this is a formidable real-life test of the effects of private administration on the wealth of a country. The East India Company transferred power to the British throne in the middle of the nine-teenth century, but the result was supposed to be a com-petitive economy. Free trade would be distilled to crystal transparency, with all barriers and tariffs eliminated. A contract signed in Bombay would have the same validity as a contract signed in London. What happened to the Indian economy as a consequence of the purest free trade regime? The result was disastrous. The income differential between an Indian and an Englishman increased from twofold in 1820 to tenfold in 1913. What happened?

The theoretician of international trade David Ricardo explained that commerce between nations is the mirror image of business dealings between persons: it hinges on the division of labor. An individual normally practices a single trade—one is a baker or a cobbler, but rarely does one practice the two occupations at the same time, even if one is equally predisposed. On a national scale, accord-ing to Ricardo, the same principle explains why a country must choose the sector in which it excels, not in the absolute sense, but relative to other options available to it. At the dawn of the nineteenth century, this choice seemed clear. England had to specialize in the industrial sector—particularly in textile, in which it led other nations. Other nations had, in all logic, to choose exactly the opposite, which meant "de-industrializing" and specializing in sectors (e.g. agriculture or mining) in which they had a comparative advantage with respect to England. Effectively this is what happened. As with all traditional societies, the Indian textile industry represented between 65 percent and 75 percent of the country's manufacturing activities. At the beginning of the nineteenth century, Indian textiles, especially calico, were very popular in London, accounting for nearly 70 percent of India's total exports. In the first half of the nineteenth century, the East India Company prohibited Indian textile firms from competing with English textile manufacturers in British territory. With the consolidation of England's industrial advantage and the free-trade practices that prevailed in the second half of the century, English textiles flowed into India and destroyed the local artisan class.[7] Thus, India lost ground in this industrial sector and in turn specialized in products where it had better comparative advantages: jute, indigo, and opium, the last product destined for China in exchange for tea. It was this type of traumatic experience that fostered the immense resentment poor countries have against "the interna-

tional division of labor." It seems self-evident with
respect to history that, in order to get rich, industrialization is paramount. And to industrialize against a rival as
dangerous as England was in the nineteenth century,
imposing commercial protections appeared to be necessary. This was the path Germany, the United States, and
France pursued when they industrialized. It is no surprise that at the moment of political independence, the
overwhelming majority of "developing" countries will
choose a protectionist path.

Unequal Exchange

The central question of Arghiri Emmanuel's book
Unequal Exchange is encapsulated in his observation
that "England made India her supplier of cotton and
Australia her storehouse of wool—something that, let
it be said in passing, had the effect of ruining India
but enriching Australia."[8] Why, Emmanuel asks, out of
the five former British colonies that are now the United
States, Canada, Australia, New Zealand, and South
Africa, are the first four among the world's richest countries while the last one remains poor? A horribly cynical
response comes to mind: in the first group, the indigenous populations were exterminated; in South Africa, the
indigenous population was exploited.[9] In the first case,
white people were given the means to be rich; in the
second case, black people were merely used. As an old
South African proverb goes: "Nothing changes as little as

the wage of a black man." No one went as far in an attempt to follow this intuition in all its implications than Arghiri Emmanuel did in *Unequal Exchange*, which enjoyed considerable fame in his time.

It is not the fact that they (badly) specialized in one task or another that explains the developing countries' poverty, but, according to Emmanuel, exactly the opposite: it is because they are poor and dominated that they are exploited dirt cheap. The shame for Marxist economists, who might have welcomed the publication of Emmanuel's book, depends less on the report itself than on the consequences that must be deduced from it. If the Third World worker is exploited, Emmanuel effectively adds, it seems that the perpetrator of the crime designates the guilty party: the capitalists. But the computations presented by Emmanuel (which would be rediscovered much later by economists of all inclinations) are without equivocation. There is no convincing proof that returns to capital in the form of profits are greater in poor countries than in wealthy countries. Far from then observing a tendency for international capital to flow toward the South, it is shown that capital has a much greater tendency to leave the South and go to the North. This raises a formidable question. If there is exploitation of "proletarian nations," but it does not result in capital profits, where could the excess yield have gone? In other words: Who really profits from the exploitation of the Third World?

Emmanuel offers a direct answer. If labor costs much less in the South than in the North and the profit rates are identical, from an accounting point of view, there only remains a single issue. The merchandise manufactured in the South must be sold at a very low price. Who then profits? There is only one candidate: the final consumer; that is, the consumer in wealthy countries; that is, since the marginal wage rates do not budge, the workers in the North. Emmanuel's response is simple: Through international trade, "a worker in Michigan can buy for one hour of his labor the product of an entire day's labor of his colleague living in the South." It is the working class in wealthy countries that exploits the working class in poor countries. Emmanuel discerns something very close to an observation by Friedrich Engels: "The English proletariat is actually becoming more and more bourgeois. . . . For a nation which exploits the whole world, this is of course to a certain extent justifiable."[10]

Why are incomes so high in wealthy countries while they are so low in poor countries? Here again, Emmanuel's answer is apparently straightforward. In the North, the class struggle turned to the advantage of the workers, which has not been the case in the South. "The effectiveness . . . and the outcome of collective or individual negotiation in general between wage earners and their employers, depends to a large extent upon the relation between what the workers are demanding and *what society regards, in a certain place and a certain moment, as the standard of wages.* It depends on a certain *level of attainment*, which is itself the result of past struggles and evolutions."[11] Emmanuel adds: "Once a country has got ahead, through some historical accident, even if this be merely that a harsher climate has given men additional needs, this country starts to make other countries pay for its high wage level through unequal exchange."[12] In other words, having more demands for reasons explained by history and reinforced by the union movement, the workers of the North can organize to pay, through international commerce, those in the South. Thus, it is necessary to reverse the manner in which the problem of global commerce is usually posed. It is not because it exports wood that Sweden has the highest standard of living in Europe. On the contrary, it must be said that Swedish wood is expensive because it is produced in a country where the working class—following given historical and political circumstances—achieved remarkable social benefits. In response to the question why, of the five former British colonies discussed earlier, only South Africa remained poor, Emmanuel says that the explanation follows directly from his theory. In South Africa, manpower remained indigenous—proletariats that the whites relegated to the ghettos. "Let us suppose," he adds, "that tomorrow the South African whites were to exterminate the Bantous instead of employing them at low wages, and replace them with white settlers receiving high wages. There would certainly occur, insofar as this operation was carried out more or less brusquely, upheavals, bankruptcies, frictions of conversion and adjustment, a transition period of great difficulty; but the ultimate result would be a leap forward by South Africa. . . ."[13]

This theory is anathema. Misunderstood, it could precipitate, and indeed it did precipitate, attempts by a number of countries to unilaterally increase wages at the risk of inflation, balance-of-payments deficits, and financial crises. However, at the heart of Emmanuel's intuition is a diamond not to be thrown out: ". . . the classical centrifugal forces of diffusion have yielded place to the centripetal forces of suction and attraction toward the 'poles of growth.'" If it is acknowledged that "economic science" has since changed its position, the judgment remains remarkable.

Back to Colonialism

Arghiri Emmanuel describes the relationship between the North and the South as allowing the former to exploit economically the latter. In doing so, he repeats the same mistakes that were made when interpreting colonialism as a means for colonial powers to exploit their colonial subjects. However, a principal fact disarms the theory according to which colonialism would be a significant factor in Western wealth: the colonial powers all experienced slower growth rates than non-colonial powers. "The correlation is almost perfect," according to Paul

Bairoch.[14] Germany and the United States, latecomers to the colonial scene, experienced faster economic growth than France or the United Kingdom; Sweden and Switzerland experienced faster economic development than the Netherlands or Portugal. Better, if it dare be said: Belgium saw its growth rate slow the moment it became a colonial power, at the turn of the nineteenth century. Conversely, the Netherlands saw its growth rebound upon losing its colonial empire. Similarly, according to Bairoch, "it is very probable that one of the reasons for the relative absence of the United Kingdom from 'new' industrial sectors at the end of the nineteenth century was precisely its very great access to colonial empires."

The idea that wealthy countries got rich thanks to the exploitation of raw materials imported from poor countries is false for one simple reason: rich countries themselves have long produced said raw materials. The fate of the developing countries was already sealed when importing raw materials became the norm for the rich countries. As Paul Bairoch explains once more, on the eve of World War I, while the developed world already possessed a manufacturing productive capacity 7–9 times the global average in 1750, 98 percent of metallic ore and 80 percent of textile fibers came from industrialized countries themselves. Energy production does not escape the rule either. Until the 1930s, the developed countries produced more energy than they consumed and released a gross excess, notably coal. The biggest energy exporter was, in fact, England, the first industrialized country. It is only due to the role played by Middle East petroleum after World War II that the scheme was reversed. Even in this case, it was not until 1957 that the United States became a net energy importer. Until World War II, energy self-sufficiency was practically assured in the West,[15] whence comes Bairoch's formula that "rich countries did not need poor countries."

Trade Less Unequal Than Expected

If the mechanism described by Emmanuel was correct, it should translate to a continuous lowering of prices of products manufactured by the South relative to those made by the North, since it is in selling high and buying low that rich countries thrive; economists call this a tendency for falling terms of trade. Indeed, Emmanuel supports his demonstration with an analysis derived from a United Nations study published in 1949. The series calculated by the UN showed a 40 percent deterioration in exchange rates for countries that produced primary products from the period at the end of the nineteenth century up to the eve of World War II.

This UN study had considerable resonance. By using these results, a fair number of authors, notably in Latin America, concluded (just as Emmanuel did later) that protectionism was the only way to enrich a poor country.[16] The problem is that the statistical fact is false.

Terms of trade did not fall. Paul Bairoch, who offered the most convincing explanation of this mistake, uncovers the source of the error in the following manner. The price of a raw material has two components: what the producers earn themselves and what they add for transport costs. It was the second term that collapsed in the period under consideration. Correcting for this factor, the conclusion must be reversed: for the period covered by the United Nations' study, terms of trade in poor countries had not deteriorated but improved. A ton of Egyptian cotton, for example, bought 7 tons of American wheat in 1870; it bought 11 tons in 1929 and 40 tons in 1950.[17] The only major exception to this average rule is the price of sugar, which explains, still according to Bairoch, the reason why the unfair-trade thesis was popular in Latin America. According to Bairoch's calculations, between 1876 and 1990 the terms of trade tripled in favor of poor countries.[18] If petroleum-exporting countries are excluded, the increase is much less spectacular; the improvement is only 30 percent. And there was, excluding oil and the postwar period, a decline in exchange rates for poor countries on the order of 25 percent. This decline is too small to explain the great schism between poor and rich.

The "Cotton Mills"

It is, thus, necessary to return to the engine of unequal exchange. Why, in the nineteenth century, did poor countries not succeed at competing with rich nations? If the English got wealthy producing textiles, why didn't the Indian cotton factories (the "Cotton Mills") dethrone their English rivals, since English wages were, at the dawn of the twentieth century, more than 6 times greater than Indian wages? In other words, why weren't the Indian textile factories more competitive? This question, to which English manufacturers respond today by outsourcing their textile production to India, has long been a mystery. In 1987, Gregory Clark, contradicting the conventional ideas, commented on this example in the *Journal of Economic History*.[19]

The lack of capital and the absence of a sufficiently qualified labor force are two reasons given to explain why industry was much less productive in India than in England. As Clark showed, in the context of nineteenth-century manufacturing, neither is valid. Since the second half of the nineteenth century, nothing prevented an Indian or a Chinese entrepreneur from purchasing English or American machines. Certain businesses, such as Platt, exported up to 50 percent of their textile machines (such as the "Ring Frames"). Those sold by Platt in England are barely more numerous than those sold in Brazil or Mexico, in India or Japan. Russia was, in fact, the first Platt market, even before England itself. In the 1840s, all operational problems with an English machine took up to 10 months before the manufacturer could supply a solution. Thanks to improved communication enabled by the telegraph or undersea cables, Platt then was able to offer effective post-sale servicing of its equipment. From then on, exported machines became nearly as productive as those used in England. For each machine in use, Indian thread production was barely 15 percent less than that recorded in England.

Labor is the second factor for which deficiency comes to mind when explaining the weak performance of Indian firms. It is only lately that Indian or Chinese workers began entering factories. Professional experience was in short supply. If the percentage of illiteracy is considered, the numbers are disconcerting. In 1950, 80 percent of the Indian population was still illiterate, whereas in 1850 the United States' illiteracy rate was under 20 percent. France, which was the most backward of the "industrialized" countries, had a 40 percent illiteracy rate at the same time. In 1900, this figure was lowered to 17 percent. This explanation, which plays a large role today, was not of prime importance at the dawn of the twentieth century. At that time, tenant farmers who had come from the southern United States seeking employment in northern factories lacked manufacturing experience, and that did not curb industrialization in the US. Similarly, in Japan and in England many of the workers were young unmarried women without particular professional experience. In the cotton mills, moreover, rarely did any task require previous training. In New England, more than one-fourth of the workers employed in the mills were Polish, Portuguese, Greek, or Italian immigrants with little manufacturing experience or education. Data collected by the Senate Commission on Immigration in 1911 showed that immigrants' wages were very close to those of other immigrants. A Greek immigrant earned 80 percent of an English immigrant's wages, while at home his productivity was one-fourth than of an English worker. It was, thus, not their "intrinsic" aptitude for work or other "natural" traits that explained the weak productivity of Indian textile workers.

Consequently, it is necessary to look elsewhere. If it is neither capital nor labor that holds the key to the mystery, then it is quite simply the combination of the two. Each English laborer operated, on average, four weaving looms at a time. At the beginning of the twentieth century, the question was how to move the English worker up to six looms. Meanwhile, in India, workers operated only one loom at a time and obstinately refused to move up to two. According to one foreman: "The workers do not do anything. They could work more, but they refuse to do it. *Unless they are paid more!*" In Bombay, strikes were launched in 1928 to prevent the local textile establishments from increasing the pace. Because the Indian managers refused to increase their wages, the Indian workers refused to conform to the English cadence. And the new Soviet state would not do much better. The attempt to make Russian weavers operate three looms at a time instead of two would fail. In France, which was behind England, negotiations around the same time resulted in going from three to four looms.[20] It is possible to discover here, in part, the intuition behind Emmanuel's reasoning. There is a fundamental difference between the wageworkers' demands in the North and in the South. In the heart of capitalism, in England or in other lands populated by European peoples, the high-wage laborers are an integral part of capitalism—they push or accompany its metamorphosis. In the countries of the South, the wageworkers' demands are illegitimate from the onset. They do not evolve capitalism, they block it. They push it toward other countries or quite simply make it ebb away.

The Spirit of Colonialism

Contrary to what Emmanuel thought, it was not a greater combativeness on the part of English workers that explains why they were wealthier. At risk of pushing the paradox, it is possible to say that exactly the opposite was true—that their tolerance of a faster work pace was more accountable for this difference. Indian workers were not passively exploited; they refused to be exploited. Neither did they reject capitalism. They waited for higher wages. Why were Indian capitalists incapable of making this simple *a priori* discovery themselves, to know that human work cannot be made productive without consideration for what people say of these aspirations? Foreign experts were numerous, and that was precisely the problem.

India was, at this time, inhabited by what could be called "the spirit of colonialism," which regards the indigenous people as negligible. Albert Memmi perfectly explained what this spirit consists of in his book *The Colonizer and the Colonized*.[21] Written in 1957 to describe the colonial situation in Tunisia, this book touches the heart of the question considered here. As Memmi describes it, the colonist feels useless. He knows that he owes everything to the mother country, which nourishes and sustains him. "France is crushed under the burden of Algeria, and we now know that we shall abandon the war, without victory or defeat, when we will be too poor to pay for it," Jean-Paul Sartre wrote in his preface to Memmi's book.[22] To give meaning to his existence, the colonist must diminish the colonized by reminding him of his inferiority in every detail of life. Every attempt at revolt by the latter is not only suppressed but anticipated; it gives the colonist a unique occasion to prove his superiority and that of the "civilization" he imposed upon on the colonized. "The colonialists are perpetually explaining, justifying, and maintaining (by word as well as by deed) the place and fate of their silent partners in the colonial drama. . . . In order for the colonizer to be the master completely it is not enough for him to be it objectively. He must believe in his legitimacy."[23] This existential contempt of the colonizer clarifies perfectly, in the case of the Indian as much as the Tunisian, the reasons why it was inconceivable they would understand the wage demands of the indigent workers as legitimate. The meaning of "unequal exchange" is now clear: not the exploitation of poor workers by rich workers, as Emmanuel thought, but the refusal of the former to be treated differently than the latter, the affirmation that they are part of the same humanity.

Conclusion

The failure of Indian industrialization sheds new light on how industrialization spread to the United States and Australia. Is it necessary to cynically concur with Emmanuel that the extermination of the indigenous population was the only way to spread "progress" in these two countries? There is a common point here with the way Jared Diamond described how agricultural societies replaced hunter-gatherer societies through annihilation. It was not the fault, however, of the indigenous peoples themselves, or else it was not understood why an Indian immigrant working in New England earned just as much as an English laborer working under the same conditions. More than anything else, it was the fault of Indian capitalism itself. The principle that Henry Ford applied at the beginning of the twentieth century, which rested on the idea that greater profits could be had by increasing the workers' wages and thereby gaining their assent and cooperation, remained beyond reach in nineteenth-century India. Here is an explanation or an interpretation that allows us to understand how the diffusion of agriculture and that of capitalism obeyed radically different laws. When hunter-gatherer societies discovered agriculture, they adopted it because they recognized a useful tool for improving their way of life, or else they rejected it because in their eyes it embodied a risk to their way of life. In the first case, they set in motion a series of unforeseen effects, at times perverse, that turned their conditions of existence upside down. In the second case, they exposed themselves to the menace of the societies that made the opposite choice. The diffusion of agriculture thus proceeded through the strange pair of adherence and extermination. Capitalism was diffused differently. At first, laborers did not mount a horse that made them travel new distances. They went to the factories, often fleeing misery, to obtain employment that only paid them a subsistence wage. Adherence came after, and depended more often on conditions that were outside of capitalism: health, education, and later social security. Indian capitalism missed a historic opportunity to turn workers' aspirations into a productive force.

At the time of their independence, many poor countries tended to believe that substituting native planners for foreign capitalists would suffice to light the spark of economic growth. After the twentieth century, during which they tried the protectionist path that the theorists of Unequal Exchange showed them, they are changing their tune. Since the death of Mao and the fall of the Berlin Wall, poor countries have begun to retake their seats at the table of world capitalism. The question now is whether they will jump out of the protectionist frying pan into the globalist fire. We cannot approach this question without realizing that capitalism in wealthy countries has, once again, profoundly changed in nature.

3   The New World Economy

The Third Globalization

International trade recovered its dynamism after World
War II. Between 1950 and 2000, international trade more
than doubled its share of the world's product, and the
increase in global trade hardly suffered any interrup-
tions.[1] Despite this spectacular growth, it was not until
1973 that the amount of global trade returned, in percentage of GDP, to the level of 1913. In England's case,
these figures would not regain their turn-of-the-century
levels until the beginning of the 1980s. This demonstrates
the extent of the depression of the 1930s. It also shows
that world capitalism was very slow to return to its nineteenth-century level of intensity. In view of these statistics, it is possible to say that the 1980s opened a new cycle
of globalization. England, yesterday's great commercial
power, has now ceded its place to the United States. The
communication revolution that yesterday was typified by

Global exports of merchandise (percentage of GDP).

1850	1880	1913	1950	1973	1985	1995
5.1	9.8	11.9	7.5	11.5	14.5	17.1

the telegraph and then the telephone today is represented by the Internet revolution, which connects the entire planet's industrial activity in real time. (See table.)

This analogy, however, is misleading, at least until recently. The nature of postwar international trade is far removed from what it was in the nineteenth century. In 1913, England imported wheat and tea and exported textiles. Essentially, it traded with distant and dissimilar countries.[2] This is no longer the case today. Commerce has become principally an affair of rich countries. Europe is, in this regard, an exemplary case. The Europe Fifteen alone represent nearly 40 percent of global commerce. But two-thirds of its exports and imports are traded within Europe itself. France, Italy, the Netherlands, and England are the principal trade partners of Germany, the number one European exporter. Trade between Germany and the United States is less than Germany's trade with Belgium and Luxembourg. And the goods traded in the heart of Europe are practically identical. Renault automobiles are traded against Volkswagens, Yves Saint-Laurent clothes against those from Prada, and so on. The majority of world trade is very much like neighborhood commerce, as much for the products as for the trading partners.

Those who taught global trade theory in nineteenth-century schools would not have imagined that two identical countries, let us say France A and France B, equal in all ways, would find the least bit of interest in trading with each other. David Ricardo's great intuition starts with a simple remark, which seems universal: what one sells, practically by definition, is different from what one buys. The baker buys shoes from the shoemaker, who, in return, buys bread from the baker. Similarly, Ricardo explained, England sells textiles to Portugal, from whom it buys wine.[3] The more countries differ, in their endowments and their expertise, the more they must find products and services to trade. Ricardo and his disciples would be surprised to discover that global trade today, far from weaving ties between distant countries, is instead what brings neighboring countries even closer.

Why do France A and France B seem, against all expectations, more interested in trading with each other than with distant and, therefore, it would seem, different countries? Why does Europe's trade with North America or with all of Asia amount to less than one-seventh of its trade within its own borders? The response requires a return to the reasons why an individual chooses to become a baker *or* a shoemaker, and never both at the same time. Ricardo explained that an individual always has a comparative advantage in one activity relative to another, and that this advantage justifies specializing in a single task. Let us imagine, however, two identical people living in the same village, which is in need of a baker and a shoemaker. Regardless of whether one person or the other possesses an intrinsic advantage directing him toward one activity or another, each will be interested in specializing in something, even if it takes flipping a coin to determine who will do what. The reasoning behind this is simple, but it has nothing to do with Ricardo's intuition. It has to do with what economists call "economies of scale." Rather than work part-time as a shoemaker and part-time as a baker, it is better to specialize full time in a single activity. There is only one career to learn, and there is only one store to buy. By specializing, one achieves "economies of scale," amortizing fixed expenses and investments on a larger volume of business. One gains a comparative advantage, which will result in specialization induced by the market, instead of "inheriting" it.

It is this idea that today is at the heart of "new theories of international trade."[4] Because of economies of scale, a business established in a territory always gains by widening its sphere of influence beyond its natural boundaries. The baker of village A will try to realize a scale economy by selling his bread to villages B and C and their environs. What happens to the bakers of villages B and C? Some will disappear. If baker A is more aggressive, he will take parts of the markets that will permit him to even better amortize his costs. But if, to fully realize a scale economy, Baker A sells only baguettes, bakers B and C could try to sell other types of bread: rye, for one, brioches for the other. It is the diversity of the offerings that will nourish trade between close countries.

Imaginary Globalization

In essence, then, trade today involves similar products traded between neighboring countries whose consumers have overlapping tastes. Nineteenth-century globalization—overseas trade between dissimilar countries—developed much more slowly than the "new-style" globalization. Once commerce with other European countries is eliminated, less than 10 percent of France's GDP consists of trade with the rest of the world, including the United States and Japan. The economist Jeffrey Frankel proposed a simple calculation to illustrate this effect.[5] The American economy represents about one-fourth of the global economy. (The same is true of Europe as a whole.) If it were perfectly integrated with the world in a trivial sense, with purchases and sales indifferent to the origin or the destination of the goods traded, the American economy would buy and sell three-fourths of its goods abroad. But its purchases and its sales correspond to only 12 percent of its GDP. Taking the difference between the theoretical figure and the real figure, a ratio of 1:6 is obtained. That is, the reality is only one-sixth as large as the fiction of a perfectly integrated world. Paraphrasing Robert Solow, one could say that globalization is seen everywhere except in the statistics. French people "see" a McDonald's on every corner, American films in all the theaters, Coca-Cola in all the cafeterias, but they are apparently blind to the thousands of French cafés that serve ham-and-butter sandwiches, the bottles of Evian and Badoit, the French films featuring Gérard Depardieu, or the regional press. In wealthy countries, globalization is largely imaginary.

The Post-Industrial Economy

To understand why globalization is omnipresent in spirit whereas it is so weak in the statistics, it helps to realize that a transformation from an industrial to a post-industrial economy is under way. As an illustration of the astonishing contrast between global trade figures and the composition of employment, consider that 80 percent of global trade is in industrial or agricultural products and only 20 percent is in services. But in wealthy countries industrial and agricultural employment account for less than 20 percent of total employment, while the service sector accounts for nearly 80 percent.[6] Here is the only real parallel that can be established between yesterday's and today's globalization.[7] In the nineteenth century, globalization hastened, more than created, the transition from an agricultural society to an industrial one. Today globalization parallels the shift from an industrial society to a post-industrial one.

In France, Jean Fourastié presciently emphasized the importance of services in the economy. At the beginning of the twentieth century, a majority of the working people in the United States and in France were farmers, and the rest were divided equally between factory workers and service employees. At the moment when industry was at its height, in the 1950s, industrial employment did not exceed one-third of total employment. Since 1949, more French have been employed in the service sector than in manufacturing factories. Today 85 percent of the American working population is employed in the service sector, and in France the percentage is approaching 75. In the entire history of the world, only in nineteenth-century England did the percentage of the population employed in industry approach 50. Since 1913, however, industrial employees have been in the minority in England. Thus, it might seem odd to speak of post-industrial societies, since industrial employment was never dominant. Service-sector activities have been present since the beginning of the industrial era. If their quantitative importance grew, does that signify that there was a rupture? A number of misunderstandings revolve around this question.

Daniel Bell wanted to interpret the post-industrial society as a "knowledge society." This term usefully puts in perspective what could appear as "A Third Age" of the world economy. The first rural age, in which the land was the principal factor of production, was replaced by the industrial period, in which humans were, in their physical strength, the principal driver of economic activity—an era that Marx defined in terms of the extraction of the human value added. Today we are living a third age, in which knowledge is the principal factor of production. This description has the merit of giving the post-industrial society a historical dimension (which, moreover, is closely equivalent to "the end of history," since it is unknown what could comprise the fourth age of human societies).[8]

The economist William Baumol is another author who has theorized the third age of what we consider the post-industrial economy. According to him, the economy consists of two sectors. First, there is the "productive" sector, where technical progress and the automation of tasks allow human labor to be more and more efficient, the machine substituting for man. Second, there is a "stagnant" sector, which includes activities like playing the violin, healing a patient, and delivering pizzas—tasks that mainly always use the same component of human time. The "stagnant" sector comprises, according to Baumol, private services, public services, health care, education, and the leisure industry. Jobs in these industries accounted for one-fourth of active employment in the postwar years, more than one-half by 1980, and nearly three-fourths today. This manner of looking at things dovetails with Alfred Sauvy's, in which employment is freed from mechanized tasks and then tends or "leans" toward tasks that cannot be mechanized and for which human labor remains indispensable. This is very close to what Jean Fourastié called the "great hope of the twentieth century," foreseeing an era in which the service sector would displace industrial jobs, resulting at last in a humane economy. These two ways of defining the post-industrial economy—as a knowledge economy, according to Daniel Bell, and as a service-based economy, according to Baumol and Fourastié—are not contradictory. Taken together, they signify the end of a world in which human work on objects is seen as the proper sphere of industrial activity. It is not, however, a lack of interest in objects that designates the post-industrial society. On the contrary, Baumol notes that never has the quantity of objects at our command been as large as today. But henceforth what will have value, what will count in the price of merchandise, is no longer the time it takes to manufacture it. Henceforth, what will count will be the *conception* and the *prescription* of objects.

At one end of the value chain, there is the production of an "immaterial" product: a chemical formula for a medicine, a song for a compact disk recording, a trademark or a brand for athletic shoes or clothing. Still, the medicine is nothing without the doctor who prescribes it, and the trademark for an article of athletic clothing counts for little without the big store where one goes to desire it, compare it against others, and eventually buy it. At the other end of the value chain, we find "face-to-face" activities. These activities, which complement the immaterial goods they prescribe, are local. They pay heavy commercial rents, dependent on the places where people live. The term "globalization" is well understood only if one recognizes that it seals the unity of a local deep-rootedness and a universal uprooting.

A Pair of Sneakers

Nothing better characterizes the new world economy than Nike athletic shoes. A product conceived in the United States, manufactured in Indonesia, advertised everywhere in the world, Nike is the target of the movie *The Big One*. This film, directed by filmmaker Michael Moore, denounces the working conditions in Indonesian sweatshops. Consider in detail the price of a pair of Nikes called "Air Pegasus." These are sold for $70. How much does the person who makes them earn? Answer: $2.75 per pair. Reading this figure, one understands the astonishment of those confronted with the difference between the price paid for this pair of sneakers in Paris or New York and the wages received by those, whether in Morocco or Indonesia, who make them. Whatever is learned of the rest of the cost structure, what would it cost the final consumer to double the wages of those who make the shoes? Would it be so bad to buy the same pair of shoes for $72.75 instead of $70?

Making the shoes also requires raw materials, such as leather and rubber. And machines have to be purchased, warehouses leased, and capital investments repaid. The finished product must then be exported. In rough terms, the pair of shoes finally costs Nike $16 to produce and ship. How does the price of something that costs about $16 to produce increase to $70 when the product is sold to the customer? The answer has two parts. First, Nike undertakes expensive publicity campaigns. The cost of the promoting a pair of shoes (which includes the fees of the stars and the ad campaigns) raises the price by $4. Add to this the Nike Corporation's employees *stricto sensu* (administrators, representatives, and so on) and its capital expenses, investment payments, and warehousing costs, and the remuneration of shareholders. It is useful here to note that Nike is not a particularly profitable enterprise. The wholesale price of the shoes—the price at which Nike sells them to its distributors—is $35.50. The difference that doubles the price comes from distribution. The personnel who secure the sale have to be paid. This is in addition to the store's rent, the remuneration of the retailer's capital investment (which also includes the repayment of investments), the warehousing costs, and the returns to shareholders.

Thus, Nike's Air Pegasus shoe costs as much to produce as a social object as it costs to produce as a physical object. That is, the promotion costs just as much as the manufacturing. In light of this, it can be said that one purchases the image, or the concept, as much as one purchases the product. And thus it costs just as much to put the shoe on the consumer's foot as it costs to produce the product in the full sense of the term. In a fascinating manner, this example illustrates the "new world economy."

To what extent may the new division of labor set a new trap for poor countries that are neither conceivers nor consumers? What place is reserved for them in the new world economy? Far from allowing them to industrialize in the nineteenth-century sense, does this process not relegate them to minor tasks, without added value, far from activities that today create wealth?

To grasp what is at stake in these questions, it is more useful to distinguish between the "old" and "new" economy than to contrast industries and services. The "new economy" had its hour of glory during the Internet bull market. Amid the folly of the dotcoms, the concept partially lost its credibility. However, it established a way to think about the novelty of the post-industrial world. It could be said that the new economy is characterized by an atypical cost structure in which it is the first unit of a manufactured good that is expensive and not those that follow. Once conceived, Windows software may just as easily be sold to a small village as to the entire world; its total production cost would be increased only marginally.

The same reasoning applies to movies, which cost a lot to produce but do not cost much to (re-)distribute. This is equally true for the pharmaceutical industry, where what counts is the invention of a vaccine and not its production, and for all industries that specialize in designing or conceiving products.[9]

The economists Brad DeLong and Michael Froomkin demonstrated in an original way how the economic model of the new economy fundamentally differs from the old one.[10] The old economy relied upon a simple and essential fact: the consumer paid the producer for a service rendered. This is hardly ever the case in the new economy. Consider broadcast television. No private channel invoices the services it supplies to the consumer. It is thanks to advertisements that the channels are financed. Therefore, the sale price does not charge for the services offered by the television channel, meaning the programs themselves, but rather charges for a derived product—the consumer's supposed attention to the commercials, which have nothing to do with the chosen program. Suddenly, the television broadcaster will not want to give the program to the consumer "for his money," but will look to furnish him with the minimum required so that he does not turn his attention away from the advertisements that finance this business. This example manifestly applies to all the "business models" that the new economy tried to make thrive. When everything is free, as is now often the case with the Internet, it is still necessary to invoice something. This could be the price of the ad or the collection of certain information on the consumer's tastes, but it is never the primary product itself. As DeLong and Froomkin humorously note, the business model of the new economy renders the gift economy more effective than mercantile trade. They even cite as an example National Public Radio, which survives off the benevolent contributions of its listeners. To obtain these, it has to seduce them, convince them; this comes closer here to the common ambition of the market economy than the broadcast television channels do.

Making the customer pay for a product that is inherently free can be called the cultural contradiction of the new economy. Users of the Internet do not want to pay for it. How can money be earned under these conditions? When the videocassette recorder was invented, Hollywood studios initially were afraid. What could be done if films started to be circulate "freely"? Today, however, the major part of their profits comes from the sale and rent of videocassettes and DVDs. Where was the error? In the case of a film, as with a song or a chemical formula, once it has been made, it should circulate as much as is possible. Whatever its merits, the movie theater binds two radically distinct products: the film itself and a technique to project it. Going into a movie theater is an act of standard consumption—it's my seat and not yours that I pay for. We continue to go to the movies, to enjoy the big screen or go out with friends, just as we still eat in restaurants despite the availability of microwave ovens. Video technology made it possible to consume a film without having to rent a seat in a theater. The film could be watched freely at one's leisure, reviewed again, and lent to one's neighbors and grandparents. The product itself found a new economic equilibrium, one closer to its original nature.[11]

To be profitable, the new economy must therefore invent a "buyer's new economy."[12] Far from realizing the coming of the "perfect" market, the new relationship with the customers does everything to keep the consumer captive. Once subscribed, one becomes a prisoner of the operator, who will multiply the ways to retain you as a customer, offering, for example, bouquets of programs that must be bought in block. This illustrates the business model of the new economy. One does not just buy the Microsoft software; one subscribes to a range of related products. We are very far from being "free to choose" as Milton Friedman demanded. The new buyer's economy takes the form of accumulating information about the client, which allows a business to categorize the client's expectations and then produce a suite of adequate products closest to his preferences (credits for purchases, different subscriptions, and so on). For example, the steps taken by airlines when they instituted a policy of tariff segmentation, or "yield management," define different commercial practices according to the clientele sector, enticing the customer's fidelity with the aid of their "frequent flyer" programs, enlarged to integrated "frequent buyer" programs through partnerships with complementary offerings as diverse as chain hotel services, car rentals, and telecommunications firms. It is obviously far from a "pure" market model where a unique price will be offered to every buyer. The investments made by firms like Amazon to research, make loyal, and interact with the possible largest clientele are considerable.

With this characterization of the new economy, we can understand why it could not accommodate what economists call a regime of "pure and perfect competition," where new entrants are *a priori* welcome. If a newly conceived software product was immediately placed in competition with similar products possessing the same features, the price war between the manufacturers would make it impossible for them to recoup their development expenses. To allay the costs of research and development that are at the heart of its activities, a firm in the new economy must benefit from its revenue position. Technological revenue for some, commercial revenue for others, matters little: the businesses in the new economy cannot be competitive in the usual sense of the word. Thus, the new economy confronts analysts with a surprising paradox. Its apologists regularly acclaim it as a powerful vector of competition. In fact, the Internet marketplace, by providing abundant and cheap information, changed the deal and destroyed the revenue position forged by those who formerly collected and distributed rare information. Think of wholesalers, concessionaires, even financial intermediaries—their margins, if any remain today, are bound to shrink. The irony, all the same, is that the actors in the new economy are themselves nothing less than rivals. Whether it is Microsoft or Time Warner, the new groups display a propensity to occupy their entire market. The "new economy" does not induce entry into the reassuring world of pure and perfect competition; it uproots us from it.

An example will illustrate the nature of the setbacks of those who imagined that new technologies were going to promote competition. With the invention of cable and satellite television, hundreds of new channels appeared in living rooms. Then it was thought that the potential diversity of the offerings would crush the dominant positions. What happened? In France there are four dominant channels. Channel TF1 holds on average one-third of the market. Antenne 2 holds one-third of the remainder (that is, 21 percent of the total). Channel Three has one-third of the residual market (15 percent of the total). Channel 6 holds 6 percent of the market (that is, one-third of the remaining segment). Cable, of course, breaks the old quasi-monopoly of the first channel. Instead of one or two players, there are at present three or four. However, the infinite diversity promised by the first prognosticators is still far away. It is on the side of the infinitely small that cable produced its effects. The opera enthusiast can enjoy three music channels; one can directly attend fashion shows or learn about the weather. All these are programs that hardly cost a thing to produce, but that very few people watch.

How is such a concentration of images to be explained? Why has the offered diversity not met its public? The economists' answer, notably since John Sutton's innovative work of, is offered here.[13] Under the "exogenous" effect of lowering broadcasting costs, *a priori* favorable to competition and program diversity, "endogenous" costs such as the broadcasting rights for big sporting events have exploded. Where technology permits the lowering of production costs, market forces restore and reconstitute the entry barriers. To put it schematically, TF1 retains its monopoly because it is the only one able to pay the salary of the soccer star Zidane, who becomes the principal beneficiary of television broadcast by cable or satellite. Similarly, today Hollywood produces more and more expensive blockbuster movies to keep competitors at a distance who otherwise would have been allowed to enter thanks to the democratization of technology. An essential point must, nevertheless, be highlighted. If the "new economy" restores in an endogenous manner the barriers that technology reduces, its particular structure remains—only the first unit is expensive to produce; the others cost next to nothing. Once completed, a film can be shown as many times as desired. Once the stars' salaries or the successive costs are paid, it can be shown everywhere, in a theater in the neighborhoods of Cairo as well as in Beverly Hills. A Rolls-Royce, on the contrary, could not be sold to the entire world; each one costs too much to produce, and therefore to buy, for the average person. The price to see a film can be fixed locally, in proportion to buying power, however low, of each person. "Hollywood's Imperialism," as it is called in France, does not have other sources. Hollywood shows the entire planet as many Rolls-Royces as it wants, and hardly anybody can buy one.

Center and Periphery

The caravel, then the railroad and the steamship enabled the first and the second conquest of the world. Today the Internet and the new economy of technology, information, and communication are bringing us into a "new world economy." The idea of a world economy came from Fernand Braudel and was reprised and developed by Immanuel Wallerstein. Braudel explains that there were always world economies: ". . . ancient Phoenicia . . . was an early version of a world economy, surrounded by great empires. So too was Carthage in its heyday; or the Hellenic world; or even Rome. . . . So was China, which from earliest times took over and harnessed to her own destiny such neighboring areas as Korea, Japan, the East Indies, Vietnam, Yunan, Tibet, and Mongolia. . . . Even before this, India had turned the Indian Ocean into a sort of private sea, from the east coast of Africa to the islands of the East Indies."[14] A world economy, according to Braudel, is a geographical space solidly fixed around a center, often a city (Venice, Antwerp, Amsterdam, London) in which people from rural areas sell their surplus. Such cities strive to subjugate others in order to ensure the continuity of trade. Venice imports everything, "even its water." There was also a new type of city: the medieval town, enclosed by its walls and place of production, such as Liege or Antwerp, where the belfry tells what time to go to work, to eat, or to go to sleep.

One center succeeds another, a process characterized as an "immense historical pendulum." The multiplication of centers is, in Braudel's eyes, a form of youth, when the struggle for the summit is not yet finished, or a form of decline, if the old center sees its authority contested. When the center is fixed, the world economy is presented as a series of concentric circles of declining prosperity gravitating around it. The center, everywhere and always, is hectic, congested, and polluted. The distant periphery is, on the contrary, synonymous with a life of slower rhythms. "Within the charmed circle of these thousands of small units where history passed in slow motion, lives repeated themselves from generation to the next; the landscape obstinately remained the same or very nearly so. . . ."[15] The "country" is worth ten times the township, the province ten times the "country." "Measured by the speed of transport of the time, Burgundy alone, in the age of Louis XI, would have been hundreds of times greater than the whole of France today."[16] In the concentric circles that surround the center resides a "coexistence," says Braudel, with different modes of production. Marx's idea according to which the modes of production succeed each other in history must be, according to him, "reviewed downwards." In all moments of history, we find a mélange of avatars from antiquity, feudalism, and the first agricultural societies.

The Paradox of Distance

Braudel cites the account of a Hungarian preacher returning to his country in 1618 who noted that all during his journey the price of bread declined regularly the further he moved away from London. This same trip taken today would still offer the same tendency. Going from Paris toward Spain and Portugal, a decline in wages is observed. Crossing Austria going east, we observe a corresponding decline in wages in proportion to the distance from the center. According to an estimate by Anthony Venables,[17] close to 50 percent of the inter-regional and international wage dispersion can be explained solely by geographic variables and the distance with respect to the great capitals. There are, of course, some "anomalies" (Australia, New Zealand, Japan, the United States, Singapore, Hong Kong) where "distance" alone is not sufficient to explain wealth. These examples show that the "tyranny of distance" (the title of a famous book devoted to Australia by Geoffrey Blainey) is not absolute.

It obstructs. Despite the considerable reduction in the "cost of distance" at work for two centuries, the world's economic geography remains surprisingly close to sheer geography.

Economists inclined toward these notions have announced what appears to be a surprising paradox: Far from dispersing economic life through space, the reduction of transport costs seems, on the contrary, to concentrate populations and wealth. The general reduction of transport costs enabled by the railroad, the automobile, and the telephone, over the course of the last two centuries, did not at all manage to diffuse wealth. At the dawn of the nineteenth century, France still had a multitude of production sites and weak, inefficient distribution across the entire country.[18] With the transportation revolution, a formidable polarization of space occurred. The "French desert," presented as a scandal, is in fact an illustration of a rule that seems universal: the reduction of transport costs, far from disseminating populations on a given territory, actually contributes to reassembling them. Villages disappear; small cities die at the benefit of large ones. The centripetal forces that drive the concentration seem much stronger than the contrary forces that induced the dispersion. The telephone is an example of the paradoxical effects at work. It was essential to the new urbanization of the world.[19] In effect, as cities gradually developed, the average distance between two people who lived there equally tended to increase with its growth. The telephone compensated for this inconvenience, always leaving open the possibility to meet face to face when circumstances required (having dinner with friends or holding an important meeting). Far from favoring the dispersion of activities over the whole region, the telephone thus made the increase in size of these population centers possible.

The decrease in the cost of distance seems, therefore, to sharpen the existing polarity between a center and its periphery more than reduce it. This paradox's explanation proceeds from the re-interpretation of the nature of commerce just outlined, which places scale economies at the center of the analysis. Let us imagine that two previously isolated regions find themselves suddenly connected by a railroad. The more developed region could then seize parts of the growing market, taking advantage of its scale economies. The same forces that let the baker from village A take the market from baker B are at work. Thanks to the decline in transport costs, it becomes possible to deliver merchandise to remote parts of the region without needing to manufacture it on site. If the second region is not sufficiently equipped to respond, it is quickly relegated to "primary" activities for which a size advantage has little or no effect.

If migration occurs, progressively emptying region B of its best elements, the process takes an irreversible turn. With workers relocating, it is also easier for firms situated in the prosperous region to hire, and for workers to find jobs. Knowledge and social usage of existing techniques are in this way more easily propagated. The inconveniences of bringing these activities together on one site—congestion, pollution, and higher rents—do not seem to outweigh the benefits procured by urban concentration. Economists analyzing regional inequalities verified the validity of these principles. When a high-speed train connects two cities, it is the less populated city that will suffer the consequences. In Europe, in spite of a general reduction in inequalities between countries, regional inequalities stopped decreasing 20 years ago.

Conforming to the Braudelian plan, the region that prospers is able to pay higher wages than the poorer region. The wealthier region benefits from the upstream ties that allow a firm to share the same labor market or range of subcontractors with other producers, what Albert Hirshman called the "backward linkages." It also takes advantage of "forward linkages," downstream ties furnished by the proximity of consumers and an understanding of their tastes. The diagram that results is of a polyvalent and prosperous "heart" and super-specialized but poor neighboring regions. Returning here to the problematic question that Jared Diamond outlined, it could be said that the center is defined as a place of high density. Counter to the Ricardian theory that it is good to specialize in a single task, there emerges an idea that is exactly the opposite: What is good for an individual is not good for a region or a nation. It is necessary to be able to rely on the services of a nearby computer maker if one is going to use these devices. One wants to benefit from a diversified range of openings if one is on the job market. It is the privilege of the center to have such a variety of choices, the curse of the periphery to be deprived of these same things.

The same logic of polarization between center and periphery is at work in urban concentrations. Since the Roman Empire, the same amount of time is required for a worker, an artisan, or a peasant to go from home to the workplace. With the commuter rail—I do not dare say "thanks to" it—the same transport time takes workers further away from city centers. The workers' cities are now so far from the center that they will never again be overtaken by the city, whereas yesterday the suburbs were progressively absorbed by urban growth. With commuter rail services, inhabitants in urban areas can go into the city center on a Saturday night to go to the movies or to restaurants. For example, the exits of the Paris commuter rail, the RER, in the city center—such as, Les Halles or the Champs-Elysées—are the suburbs' connections during the weekend. This signifies in turn that these suburbs will never become entirely separate towns with a "normal" public space. These suburbs are bedroom communities; the life of the town is lived elsewhere.

Zara and Barbie

The dissociation between the center and the periphery is equally at work in the productive domain. If we take the example of financial services, there exist back offices and front offices, long lodged in the headquarters of big banks. Located in London or New York, the front offices are characterized by a particularly strong concentration of high-value added personnel. Thanks to the Internet, the back offices can be relocated anywhere, in Senegal or Morocco for example, in the French case. In the same manner, American telephone service calls are placed to the Philippines to ensure their overnight availability— thanks to the time difference, they offer, in effect, 24-hour service. The Philippine telephone centers can give directory information, and can transcribe medical prescriptions for hospitals and care centers. The difference in time zones lets doctors leave their medical reports in the evening and find them transcribed the next morning.[20] The doctors remain in New York, their secretaries can be in Bombay. The center/periphery dichotomy is inscribed at the very heart of the productive process.

The Internet allows for a subtler dialectic, however. The information society permits, in effect, flexible production, "just in time," and "made to order."[21] No longer is a firm concerned about producing first and selling later; now there is a constant give-and-take between production and consumption, where the customer practically becomes the one who gives production orders. Zara is a perfect example. Its founder, Amancio Ortega, was one of the pioneers of in using new technologies in the retail apparel industry. While The Gap follows the regular model of four design collections per year, Zara's stock is updated every other week. The time between conception and execution is five weeks at Zara, whereas at The Gap there is a nine-month delay. Zara's performance is the work of an "armada" of 200 designers who produce 12,000 different designs each year. The basic business model is to play on the consumer's impatience. If she likes a product, the customer must purchase it right away or risk never finding it again. Zara manages fashion in real time, the tastes of consumers are a function of sales. Sales are tied to an ultramodern factory in Spain's Galicia region. If blue does not sell, Zara switches to red. Zara has plenty of inventory, but of raw textiles, not clothing. Its stores, except those in New York, receive deliveries by truck.

Zara exemplifies a unique manner of combining the advantages of being close to the center and the final consumer, and being able to count on a relatively cheap workforce. It locates its factories in a still peripheral zone of Europe, the Galicia, sufficiently close, nevertheless, to be a quick distance from the stores. This permanent dilemma between staying near the "center," where it is expensive, and production in the "periphery," where everything costs less, is a constant tension in the market economy. Already in the eighteenth century, the countryside competed with the cities, in a process that came to be called proto-industrialization, which outlined the high prices of the cities and the power of artisan co-operatives, the guilds, that retained a monopoly on their craft. How far can be removed to combine the advantages of flexibility and avoid the inconvenience of higher costs? Zara chose a middle road, but the scope remains large. Multinational firms also hesitate between these two models. For a long time they tried to simulate a promising market.[22] McDonald's established itself in France not to sell its products (produced locally) but its brand and way of doing things. Essentially, it is the consumers of the countries where they choose to locate that principally interest these multinational firms. For a long time, their direct foreign investments were principally directed toward wealthy countries. This is still the case today, even if the first recipient of foreign investment is now China. Likewise, the larger the direct investments toward a country, the higher the recipient country's customs barriers: on-site investments are a manner of overcoming the tariff obstacle and reaching the client. At the beginning of the 1980s, Japanese automobile firms multiplied their investments in the United States to avoid the Americans' protectionist policies.

Since the mid 1980s, this pattern has been in constant evolution. The multinationals have established themselves in countries where customs tariffs are low so as to use those countries as platforms for re-exportation. In

East Asia, on average 50 percent of the multinational firms' production is re-exported. This re-exportation takes place within an increasingly sophisticated chain of production. The Barbie doll offers a shocking model of what is called "vertical disintegration" of the manufacturing process. The raw materials, the plastic and the hair, come from Taiwan and Japan. Assembly takes place in the Philippines before moving to regions with lower wages, such as Indonesia and China. The molds come from the United States. The final painting is done in the US.[23] The opposite of Zara's integrated production and consumption, Barbie pushes the search for the lowest cost to the extreme by recourse to generalized subcontracting.[24]

However, nothing better illustrates in every way these two temptations of globalization—distant yet cheap production, or closer but more expensive—than the rivalry between Mexico and China. The North American Free Trade Agreement (NAFTA), signed in 1994, designated Mexico as the main subcontractor of the United States. Since this accord, Mexico has in fact become a platform of re-exportation thanks to the so-called *Maquiladoras*. In 1982 only 10 percent of production by American firms established in Mexico was re-exported to the United States. Since NAFTA, it has been the case for 40 percent of their local production. The majority of Mexican employment today is situated on the US border, whereas in the 1980s it was principally located in various regions of Mexico. Following what can be called the Zara model, the American multinationals import 30 percent of their Mexican or Canadian affiliates' needs. But China, more distant but much cheaper, has experienced a parallel evolution. In the early 1980s, the multinationals located in China exported only 20 percent of their production. This figure has since doubled.[25] The current debate revolves around to what extent China is prepared to dislodge Mexico from the position it acquired after great difficulty. Despite being "24 hours by truck" from its American clients, Mexico feels threatened. It fears that China's east coast will become the world's workshop. We have here an illustration of "concentrating" forces in a country of the South. But China itself is trying to organize a new center-periphery duality between its urbanized east coast and its 800 million poor peasants. The inequality between the two groups has nearly doubled in 20 years, going from a ratio of 1:2 to a ratio of 1:4. The South-South tension here promises to be at least as intense as the tension between the North and the South.

Conclusion

The simple lesson that Mexico is learning anticipates what China may learn one day: that a country cannot hope to prosper solely on the basis of the international division of labor. Just as yesterday the industrialization of rich countries was responsible for the South's poverty, the deindustrialization of advanced economies will not by itself create tomorrow's prosperity in the developing world. In order to grow, a country must become a "center" in its own right; that is to say, a place dense with production and consumption. Because the new economy gives rise to the illusion of a world without borders, it fosters the hope that the North-South tension is going to be resolved. However, reducing the costs of distance does not bring either people or wealth any closer. It tends, moreover, to heighten the polarity between the center and the periphery, in the image of the town center and its suburbs. Contrary to the Braudelian plan, according to which the periphery lives a "history [that passes] in slow motion, lives repeat themselves from generation to the next," the suburban life illustrates the novelty of the new world economy. Through the commuter railway or the movies, the suburbs of Paris, Cairo, Mexico, and China all evenly gaze upon the world. It is the world which ignores them.

4

The Clash of
Civilizations?

The Clash of Populations

According to projections by the United Nations, the
world will have 9 billion inhabitants in 2050, as compared
to 6 billion today. Half of this projected population
increase will be concentrated in six countries: 21 percent
in India, 12 percent in China, 5 percent in Pakistan, 4
percent each in Bangladesh and Nigeria. The United
States, the only rich country in this group, will grow by
4 percent. India and China, between them, will account
for more than one-third of the global population. The
only continent that will have a decrease in the absolute
number of inhabitants will be Europe; it will have 630
million people, as opposed to 730 million today.[1] Over the
course of the next 50 years, 90 percent of the world's new
inhabitants will come from poor countries. The African
population will double by 2050, despite deplorable sanitary conditions and the effects of AIDS. There will be

1.8 billion Africans in 2050, compared to 850 million today.

For "us Westerners," the only possible development model seems to be one accompanied by a transition from high to low fertility. Economic development as we understand it takes place in a sequence whereby greater wealth increases the income of individuals, not their numbers. This shift requires two essential changes, regarding people in general and women in particular. Aside from the level of health care afforded to individuals, education is the chief factor necessary for a transition to where the "quality" of life is substituted for the "quantity," as given in the provocative formula used by the economist Gary Becker. The place of women in a given society is one of the main variables upon which these changes can be directly gauged. Amartya Sen drew economists' attention to what has been called the problem of "missing women."[2] In population statistics for poor countries, we find a disturbing shortage of women, which indicates the violence they encounter.

Few debates are as lively as the one that deals with "demographic transition," a process by which the birth rate decreases. Very little has changed since the conclusion by the United Nations to which Paul Bairoch referred: that "the empirical and comparative study of the interrelation between population and economic growth remains one of the least explained areas in the field of demographic economic interrelation."[3] Economists disagree violently about whether there is a causal connection. Does demography cause poverty by forcing countries to drain their scarce resources to feed surplus populations, despite Mao's dictum that a mouth more to feed means two more hands to work? Or does poverty engender a demographic explosion, as the only precautionary saving available to poor families is having their own children to help them face the hazards of existence? This debate is quite important, but the results do not depend on the answer that we supply. When it is all said and done, the highest birth rates are indeed found in the most impoverished regions of the world. For whatever reason, the number of poor people tends to increase.

If we are inquiring into the forces at work, it is easy to caricature the effect of high population growth as either suggesting that the demographic explosion is killing economic growth or, inversely, that there is no correlation between demography and prosperity. Neither are right. "Optimists" are too easily reassured, and "alarmists" are too quickly disquieted. Siding with the optimists, one can certainly appeal to global statistical relationships that show no significant correlation between demographic growth and per-capita income.[4] The idea that strong demographic growth is always synonymous with poverty is not true. In Asia, where we observe the world's strongest per-capita income growth, population growth is among the fastest. Among the middle-income countries, we find Argentina (where income and population growth are both low) but also Botswana (where income and population growth are increasing simultaneously). Finally, in the world's advanced nations, demographic growth and economic growth have been declining for 30 years.

But it is difficult to fault Bairoch's remarks regarding how much expanding poverty in Third World cities is associated with an unprecedented population explosion.[5] Between 1950 and 1990, the population of the Third World increased twice as rapidly as that of the rich countries during their period of maximum growth. Shantytowns proliferated, and in 1980 they housed 40 percent of the poor countries' urban populace. According to the United Nations, cities in the South will go from having 2.8 billion inhabitants in 1990 to 5.8 billion by 2025. In the countryside, the figures are no less alarming: the rural population in the poor countries is also increasing at an impressive pace, which is worsening the already unfavorable balance between the agricultural land available and the burgeoning population. Around 1950, an agricultural worker in a poor country did not have more than 6 acres of agricultural land, while in Europe the comparable historic minimum has been just below 9 acres. In the United States, the corresponding figure is 36 acres. In the developing world, this amount decreased in 1990 to just below 4.5 acres per worker (and just under 1 acre in Bangladesh). Some of these figures give an idea of the size of the phenomenon. For example, Egypt's population is increasing at a dizzying pace. In 1913 Egypt had 13 million inhabitants. Today it has 70 million, and it is going to surpass 100 million by 2025. But only 4 percent of Egypt's land is arable. Cairo alone has 23 million inhabitants. Brazil is another example: its population was 52 million people in 1950; in 2000 it was 170 million.

Bairoch remarked on the improbable coalition between the Marxists and the Roman Catholic Church, an alliance founded on their shared opposition to birth control. The Catholic Church is known for its general opposition to contraception, while the Marxists invoke the argument regarding the self-impoverishment of workers that pitted Karl Marx against Thomas Malthus. The historical irony is that reputedly Marxist countries, such as China and Cuba, are among those that have imposed the most severe controls on reproductive freedom. Such coercive measures are seldom enacted by governments concerned with "human rights."

Can the demographic transition be exported? Or is it better to give up and admit that here is the heart of what Samuel Huntington termed "the clash of civilizations,"[6] acknowledging the inability of certain societies to stop exploiting women? The answer is simple: the transition has already begun. All over the world, and particularly in poor countries, the birth rate is plunging toward the threshold reproduction rate of 2.1 children per woman. The decline in reproduction is most impressive in im-poverished regions. Where this is happening, on average, there were 6 children born per woman in 1950 and 5 in 1970, but 4 in 1980 and 3 today. This most important trend at the start of the twenty-first century remains singular in its novelty, unrecognized except among specialists. Most of the 143 countries making up the group of poor nations have for 30 years experienced a birth rate greater than 5 children per woman. Today this is the case in no more than 49 countries, while 21 of the remaining countries have already registered a birth rate well within the replacement rate.[7]

No religion is exempt from these effects. In Brazil, a devout Catholic nation with a historically high birth rate, in less than 20 years the reproduction rate has gone from 4 children per woman to 2.3. Between 1950 and 2000, Egypt saw its birth rate drop from 7 children per woman to 3.4; Indonesia went from 5.6 to 2.6. In India, over the same period, the birth rate declined from 6 children to 3.3 children. By dubious methods, to be sure, at 1.8 children per woman now China is below the replacement birth rate. What is the reason for this colossal drop? The experts emphasize the importance of economic development and education, most notably of girls.[8]

Women's education is supposed to lead to career opportunities, which act to reduce or delay births. Independent of the economic benefits, women's participation in the labor market is a factor in their declining fertility, which gives them a new autonomy that allows them to oppose patriarchy. Nevertheless we observe in these facts a demographic decline even though the number of countries affected by this trend remains in the minority. Not only are these changes occurring in the countryside as well as in the cities, but these changes are of equal concern in those countries where women's participation in the labor market is still weak. At the same time, indicators of human development such as education, even if these partially help in forecasting the speed of the demographic transition, remain weak, indeed non-existent, in predicting when it actually will take off.

Today Africa is the only continent where demographic growth is too quickly outstripping resources. As we have seen, the number of Africans will double in the next 50 years. The birth rate is still projected to remain at 5 children per woman, slightly below earlier figures. Yet other very impoverished countries, including Nepal, Bangladesh, Haiti, and Guatemala, escape this rule. One notable exception of a country outside Africa that still has a high fertility ratio is Pakistan, which perhaps explains the misunderstandings of "Islamic" demography. Pakistan's birth rate remains at 5 children per woman.[9] Despite these exceptions, the demographic transition, understood as a shift to a birth rate below 2.1 per woman, nonetheless will be achieved, according to the United Nations, in 75 percent of the world's countries by 2050.

The experts at the United Nations who have been considering this question were thus obliged to revise their doctrines.[10] The drop in fertility seems to be explained more by the diffusion of cultural behavior than by the economic theory of cost-benefit analysis. The number of television sets is a better predictor of the demographic decline than the level of revenue or education. The changing behavior is more attributable to the new reference models that people want to adopt than to the material reality of the countries where they reside. For example, young Chinese women try to emulate the low fertility of young Japanese women.[11] The demographic transition came about faster in Brazil (where there were no family-planning policies) than in Mexico (where family planning was important). In poor countries, behavior advances ahead of material reality.

The demographic transition is directly related to the "clash of civilizations." The opposition between a patriarchal society and a "modern" society as we in the West understand it often has to do with the status of women. That women have freed themselves from the authoritarian patriarchal model (at least by the standard of this indicator) must count for something in our diagnosis of the advance of civilizations. The question is whether this discrepancy between behavior and conditions of existence can last long.[12]

What Went Wrong?

In *The Clash of Civilizations and the Remaking of the World Order*, Samuel Huntington places Islam at the center of the declared war between religions. According to him, Islam poses a demographic threat. However, we saw that the demographic transition did not spare Muslim countries. But with Islam representing 20 percent of the world's population and only 6 percent of its wealth, the temptation to conclude that Islam does not square well with economics in particular or with the modern world in general is irresistible. The Islamic case is only one variant of a problem that has been posed a thousand times. The idea that religion can have a predictive power on the material prosperity of societies is due to Max Weber's book *The Protestant Ethic and the Spirit of Capitalism*. Along with others, Weber gave the impetus to such consideration by asking about "the influence of certain religious ideas on the development of an economic spirit, or the *ethos* of an economic system."[13]

To observe that the Muslim population is poorer than the global average, however, is not sufficient to conclude that we have found a causal relationship between the first and second term, no more than one would like to wager today that its Confucian heritage is responsible for China's poverty or would dream of pitting Catholicism against Protestantism in order to understand the differences in wealth between nations.[14] However, all these observations were made in the past. It was explained that, if Japan prospered and China did not, this was due to the fact that Shintoism, a "local version of Protestantism," was imposed on the Land of the Rising Sun, whereas Confucianism (closer to Catholicism?) dominated the Middle Empire.[15] Now that China fires up its industrial production and its economic growth is nearly 10 percent per year, we no longer know what to think of the power of these theories to understand what determines the aptitude to embrace capitalism. In the same way, Ireland, Portugal, and Spain, devout Catholic countries, belatedly boarded the train of economic growth, but Ireland has already passed the European average, and there is no doubt that Spain and Portugal will achieve this goal and catch up to the living standards of most advanced European countries. Neither Confucianism nor Catholicism was able to pose a strong obstacle to capitalism for very long.

If previous errors in reasoning warn us against hasty extrapolations, in the meantime we cannot dispense with taking up the problem with respect to Islam. To settle this question "scientifically," it would be necessary to command useful points for comparison. Economists want to judge the specific importance of a given factor by reasoning that "all other things remain equal." Most often, the task is impossible. As opposed to the experimental sciences that apportion the concentration of such and such variable in order to judge its effects, economists most often must consider all parameters together. Milton Friedman remarked, however, that the enterprise is not always vain, and that history is replete with episodes that look like "natural" or "controlled experiments." Friedman suggested that anyone who wants to judge the superiority of a market economy over a planned economy need only compare North Korea to South Korea, East to West Germany before the fall of the Berlin Wall, or China to Taiwan. The same initial conditions are present, as well as the same history and the same people, yet at the end an indisputable difference between the two regimes.[16]

To which countries must the development of Muslim nations be compared? The answer is simple: to their non-Muslim neighbors. While it is ridiculous to compare Islam in general to the rest of the world, it is not unreasonable to compare a Muslim country to a close neighbor that is not Islamic. What do we observe if, for example, we compare Malaysia to Thailand, Senegal to the Ivory Coast, or Pakistan to India? The first examples all have a Muslim majority, while the others have populations half or more of which follow non-Islamic religions. The result is clear: only a small difference or none is apparent. Malaysia has an annual per-capita income of $6,990, Thailand $5,840, Senegal $1,750, the Ivory Coast $1,730, Pakistan $1,540, and India $1,700. Viewing these figures, it is difficult to conclude that Islam is a prime factor in economic growth. We can extend this comparison to other indicators of human development, life expectancy, and education. The similarities are mores striking than the differences. Indonesia, the world's most populous Muslim country, is in fact the country with the region's second-lowest birth rate (after Thailand), reaching a level of 2.6 children per woman in 2000. Indonesia's birth rate was twice as high in the early 1960s. The Philippines, a nearby predominantly Catholic country with a slightly higher income, has a birth rate of 3.6 children; India's birth rate is 3.

How do we understand the influence of geographic proximity as opposed to the role played by different religions? We can think of commercial trade and migration. The same mechanisms of diffusion of behavior can explain that the demographic transition is undoubtedly the most powerful influence. When a neighboring country attempts something that succeeds, one inevitably ends up doing the same thing. Regional trading blocks seem to manifest a tendency toward convergence. Western Europe, very diverse at the end of the nineteenth century, exhibited clear convergence at the dawn of the twenty-first century. If we judge it by the performance of Chile, Argentina, and Brazil, South America is experiencing a similar fate. The same trend is true in Asia today. The same was true in the nineteenth century, when the Industrial Revolution, which began in England, reached France and then Germany before touching, nearly a century later, Christian Russia, where it dried up. Similarly, nothing was more important for Asia than the success of Taiwan or South Korea, and nothing would be more important for Africa than the success of South Africa or Nigeria.

These comparisons will not suffice to convince the skeptics. They could respond that these examples were chosen in an arbitrary manner with the aid of hindsight. But this is not the case. Over the course of the twentieth century, no statistically significant differences existed between Muslim nations and their neighbors in matters of economic growth. What economists have learned from the wealth of nations is the importance of geography. There is no better predictor of a country's economic growth than the rate of growth of its immediate neighbors. It is Africa (in general) that has a problem, not Islamic Africa compared with the rest of the continent. It was Asia that experienced a financial crisis in 1997, not Malaysia or Indonesia compared to Thailand or the Philippines. And, returning to the question at hand, it would be wiser to speak of Central Asia or the Middle East than of Islam in general.

Mohammed and Confucius

In *What Went Wrong?* Bernard Lewis also asks what delayed the economic development of today's Muslim societies.[17] How do we understand that this civilization, very advanced compared to the West at the start of the second millennium, lost ground between the sixteenth and the seventeenth century? "At the peak of Islamic power," Lewis writes, "there was only one civilization that was comparable in the level, quality, and variety of its achievements; that was of course China."[18] Islam was constantly passing between the West and East. From China it exported paper to the West, and from India it borrowed the decimal system. The guardian of the Library of Alexandria, it saved the history of Greek philosophy. "In most of the arts and sciences of civilizations, medieval Europe was a pupil and in a sense a dependent of the Islamic world. . . ."[19] In *The Lever of Riches*, a history of technology, the economic historian Joel Mokyr also recalls the variety of loans the West received from the Islamic world.[20] In the agricultural domain, Muslims taught the West how to master complex irrigation systems. It supplied the West with rice, durum wheat, oranges, lemons, bananas, watermelon, asparagus, artichokes, spinach, and eggplant. In the industrial sector, Muslims were particularly advanced in textile production. They introduced cotton to the West. Leather and metallurgy were also among their specialties.

Then the relationship between the two civilizations was suddenly reversed. Even before the Renaissance, the Muslims admired the Europeans for making serious progress in art and culture. During the Renaissance, they made great advances, leaving the scientific, the technological, and even the cultural heritage of the Muslim world far behind. According to Lewis, the problem was not the Islamic world's decline. The Ottoman Empire and its armed forces were just as effective as they had always been, in traditional terms. In this regard, as in many others, it was the inventiveness and dynamism at work in Europe that increased the gap between the two groups. The Middle East had no problem importing the cannon, the musket, and the telescope from the West. But that was all. Later, however, "the Renaissance, the Reformation, the technological revolution passed virtually unnoticed in the lands of Islam."[21] It was only slowly, toward the end of the eighteenth century, that "knowing how to talk to and deal with Europeans, knowing what was going on in Europe" became positive assets for an Ottoman.[22] But it was too late. The West's ascension took the Muslim world by surprise.

This destiny of Islam that seems so particular is really not original. We observe almost the same process in China. At first open to and curious about the rest of the world, China suddenly closed itself to the rest of the world at the same time that Europe began its ascension. The popular image of a China shut in upon itself and with mistrust receiving foreign merchants was only true after the sixteenth century. In 1137, the Emperor Kao Tsung explained it this way: "The profits from commercial shipping are very important. Managed correctly, it can yield millions—is this not preferable to the previous taxes imposed on the people?"[23] This policy denoted a new spirit under the Mongolian Dynasty (1280–1368). Foreign merchants were welcomed. Sustained by the introduction of a new efficacious variety of rice, which rapidly matured and permitted two or three harvests per

year, China entered a prosperous economic period close
to that which the European countries would experience
in the eighteenth century. A policy of stockpiling grain
was instituted in order to avoid famines. Paper currency
was reestablished and became the sole legal tender.
Canals were dug and coastal traffic developed. It was
during this period that Marco Polo's famous voyage took
place.

At the dawn of the fifteenth century, decades before
Christopher Columbus launched his three fragile ships
across the sea, China dispatched fleets of several hundred
ships about 400 feet long and with crews totaling 28,000
across the Indian Ocean to the eastern coast of Africa.
In 1490, however, just before Columbus discovered
America, the Chinese decided to stop these expeditions
and enacted measures closing their country to foreigners.
The doors of the Celestial Empire were suddenly closed
after a palace revolution that pitted the eunuchs, who
favored openness, against the Imperial Court, which
opposed it. The society remained prosperous, but its
decline began.[24] Commenting on the episode, Jared
Diamond noted that in China a decision at the top was
sufficient to interrupt an entire chain of development. On
the contrary, in Europe, a pioneer such as Christopher
Columbus could endure five failures before convincing
a European prince, among hundreds, to finance him.
Thanks to this political fragmentation, and not in spite of
it, Europe proved to be a land open to innovation. The

same scenario would be repeated with the development of the cannon, the electric light, the printing press, and other innovations. In certain parts of Europe, each of these novelties was at first neglected (if it did not incite downright hostility for idiosyncratic reason)s, but as soon as it was adopted in one place it spread across the rest of the Continent. Because China made one decisive move to isolate itself, a long period of closing began after 1490; it ended only in 1842, with the Treaty of Nanking, under which England obligated China to open its ports to the opium trade.[25] Beginning in1872, China became a semi-colony. The Boxer Rebellion began in February 1900 and ended in September 1901 after being quelled by Western powers.

Conclusion

Until 1450, China was much more innovative than Europe. We are indebted to it for it "water locks, cast-iron, deep drilling, armor, gun powder, kites, the magnetic compass, paper, porcelain, printing, the rudder, and the wheelbarrow."[26] Then the innovation ceased. As with Islam, China closed itself off at the same moment that Europe ascended. This decoupling preceded the English Industrial Revolution. Contrary to what Paul Bairoch thought, Europe's per-capita income had already surpassed China's and India's on the eve of nineteenth-century globalization. According to Angus Maddison

(today's authority), the ratio was already $1:2$ in 1820.[27]
The entire history of the nineteenth century would see
this gap get wider, not because India became impoverished, but because it would not succeed at following
British prosperity. However, in 1948, Chiang Kai-Shek
fled the continent and settled in Taiwan. Fifty years later,
Taiwan's standard of living has nearly reached the
English level. It is possible to say that continental China
simply wants to be like Taiwan. And it is difficult to find
"cultural" reasons why it could not attain this. Any
analysis based on religious or cultural reasons why the
Chinese or Muslims have lagged behind the West run the
risk of being contradicted when each of the political
regimes identified with these two civilizations changes
course.

5

Indigenous Growth

The Quest for the Grail

After decolonization, the idea that nothing should pose an obstacle to the prosperity of the newly independent countries became popular. In *The Elusive Quest for Growth* (MIT Press, 2001), the economist William Easterly cites Ghana as an example of the disillusion that the end of colonialism brought.

In 1957, when Ghana gained its independence from England, it produced two-thirds of the world's cacao. It had the best schools in Africa. Health services were good. At the inauguration of President Kwame Nkrumah, excitement and hope were palpable. Soon after he came to power, Nkrumah called for Ghana to begin building an integrated aluminum industry. A large hydroelectric dam would supply electricity to a huge complex that would feed the chain of production, supporting aluminum production and other industries. Experts offered encouragement, adding that a dam would create a fishing industry. With support from the British and American governments and from the World Bank, the Akomboso Dam was built. On May 19, 1964, in a grandiose ceremony, President Nkrumah opened its gates. After some delay, the aluminum factory was also built.

Forty years later, Ghana was hardly any richer than it had been in 1957. Aluminum production, on average, grew 1.5 percent per year between 1969 and 1992. But not a single positive "externality" was manifested, and everything bad that could happen did happen. The fishing industry did not materialize. The Akomboso Dam multiplied the incidence of malaria and schistosomiasis. In 1966, Nkrumah was overthrown in a coup d'état—the first of five that would took place in 15 years. When Nkrumah was ousted, the crowds were overjoyed. His pharaonic projects had starved the capital, Accra, and had precipitated inflation. The Ghanaians would have been less enthusiastic had they known what was in store for them. The army restored democracy for two years, from 1969 to 1971, under President Kofi Abrefa Busia; then the army got rid of him. In the 1970s, famine reappeared. At the beginning of the 1980s, the average income in Ghana was one-third below its 1971 level, reaching a low point in 1983 during a drought that rendered the Akomboso Dam useless. That same year, the Ghanaians received only two-thirds of the calories deemed necessary for a normal diet. Malnutrition was responsible for half of the infant mortality. In 1983, the average income was below what it had been in 1957.

Many technical errors explain this disaster, and Ghana is only one example among many aborted investment strategies. William Easterly cites as another example Tanzania, where a new shoe factory, financed by the World Bank, was supposed to supply the entire Tanzanian market and make it possible to export 4 million pairs of shoes to Europe.[1] Owned by the Tanzanian government, the factory never used more than 4 percent of its production capacity. It was not adapted to the Tanzanian climate; it had aluminum walls and had no ventilation system. Other African "white elephants" during the years of "development" are well known. Economists did not lack theories to explain the failure of the strategies followed, after the fact. They first invoked the role of human capital, more so than physical capital, as a key to growth. Then it was about technical progress, institutions, and business confidence as crucial factors for development. The deception was repeated each time.

In his way education has also disappointed expectations. Between 1960 and 1990, Nepal raised the percentage of an age group receiving a primary school education from 10 percent to 90 percent. Its economic growth, however, remained pathetically weak. Angola, Ghana, Jordan, Madagascar, Mozambique, Senegal, and Zambia also experienced an apparently spectacular increase in their education levels. In those nations where education grew more than 4 percent per year, per-capita income growth languished at less than 0.5 percent a year. In the 1990s when the most spectacular efforts were made in matters of education, growth was weaker than it had been in the five preceding decades. As in the case of the aluminum factories that someone forgot to furnish with air conditioning, naturally there would be much to say about the educational content itself. In Pakistan, according to Easterly, 75 percent of teachers would not have passed the exams they made their students take.[2] The position of instructor was the result of political nepotism. Much was spent on the teachers' salaries, and hardly anything on the rest of the necessary educational infrastructure. According to the economists Lant Pritchett and Dean Filmer, allowances for other expenditures, such as books and pencils, should be 10 times what is spent on teachers.[3] It is evident that the world's best intentions are often turned away from their purpose in corrupt societies. Such is the principle lesson of the failures that followed decolonization: no development project is ever effective if it is not supported by the society. Development strategies established by some experts in an office are almost fatally condemned to failure. In their own fashion these are repetitions of the colonial style.

The Japanese Model

Among the poor countries, the perspective regarding failures recorded after independence changed with the diffusion of a development model originating from Asia. A series of coups d'état brought "pro-business" authoritarian regimes to power. This was the case in Malaysia in 1958, in Thailand in 1960, in South Korea in 1961, and in Indonesia in 1966. In all these instances, the powerful hand of the state was present, and together with development banks the state contributed to the financing of great infrastructures—electrification, highways, airports. In Thailand, the Board of Investment was involved with nearly 90 percent of industrial projects.[4] It was there to offer tax breaks and loan subsidies.[5] For all these countries, the model to imitate is the only non-Western country to have succeeded in catching up to the West: Japan.

Japan is a fascinating example. With China and the Islamic world, it once was one of the world's most closed societies. From 1639 to 1854, only one Western ship per year was authorized to enter a Japanese port. Then came the famous episode in 1854 when, from the bridge of his cruiser, Commander Perry forced Japan to open its ports. The first moments following this shock were similar to the economic transition experienced by the Eastern Bloc in the 1990s after the fall of the Berlin Wall. Japan recorded a sixfold increase in prices between 1859 and 1865. Its political power vacillated. The *shogun* disbanded and the emperor retook the reins. The decision to modernize the country was made in an instant, without a transition phase, in what could be called "shock therapy." This was the Meiji Revolution of 1868, begun by agrarian reforms that emancipated the peasants. They were declared proprietors of their land, taking care, however, to avoid the pauperization of the most vulnerable by prohibiting the sale of land until 1872, a measure still imitated today by China.[6] An enlightened reform of real estate taxes was undertaken, replacing proportional taxes with lump sum ones. The government intervened in the sectors where private initiatives were judged as weak, but only for a limited time, and these businesses were sold at the end of a few years. In return, the privatizations gave the state the financial means to take action in other areas. The government shared in the initiative to import foreign machinery. An example of each kind was exhibited from district to district to serve as models for the local mechanics. Finally, Japan sent numerous technicians abroad, but only occasionally brought in foreign technicians.[7] A radical transformation in education was also undertaken. In 1913, the rate of industrialization (per inhabitant) was less than 45 percent of that in Europe. By 1938, Japan had become the world's fifth-largest industrial power.

In Asia a century later, the model has remained almost the same. Industrialization under the aegis of different development banks was carried out at once by different subsidies, such as government tax breaks and subsidized loans. But contrary to what happened in Ghana, for example, the firms receiving government aid were always part of a measurable objective, most often in matters of exports. If an enterprise failed to meet its targets, it was immediately stripped of its credits. It is this repeated insistence on exports that indicates the fundamental difference between the Asian and Latin American development models. Perhaps unconsciously, Latin America wanted to replicate the North American experience of the "great internal market." It is surprising that the average annual growth rates of Korean exports exceeded 25 percent per year, while Taiwan experienced export growth of 20 percent per year. Today more than 90 percent of both these countries' exports are industrial products.[8] China exhibits the same trend. With a ratio of export to GDP at 25 percent, China now exports 85 percent of the industrial products it manufactures.

The Role of International Trade

Global trade had no positive effect on India or China during the nineteenth century. If the attitude of these countries toward trade changed, it is largely because the protectionism they adopted afterward was hardly more beneficial. In this respect India constitutes a perfect example. Since gaining its independence in 1947, it established a policy destined to recapture its domestic market. In 1913, India was seven times poorer than Latin America, with an income close to what today would be called subsistence level. In 1990, after more than 40 years of protectionist policy, with great difficulty India attained an income equivalent to the US level of 1820, being in 1990 more than 16 times poorer than the United States in that same year. The countries already independent in the nineteenth century that had erected very high tariff barriers to protect themselves against international competition, such as Brazil and Mexico, hardly had better success. Commenting on Mexico, the economist Alice Amsden feels that it did not succeed at catching hold of a spiral of growth precisely due to protectionist reasons. Mexico's entrepreneurs preferred to share the profits from a captive market rather than innovate.[9]

These failures go well beyond the chosen trade regime. The unrealized opportunities designate a single missing factor, the absence of an interior engine of growth, that can be called "indigenous growth" (by reference to the theorist of "endogenous growth"). The question of education offers a crucial example of what forces are at play. Everywhere, under-education has remained the norm in emerging countries. Whether it was India, China, Brazil, or Turkey, in 1950 these countries averaged less than 3 years of education per adult; in Europe the corresponding figure was 8 years. Here we have one of the factors that directly elevated Japan to the rank of a great power. Every village there already had a school at the start of the nineteenth century, well before the 1868 Meiji Revolution. Since 1872, primary school has been a general requirement.[10] In 1937, the effective difference in higher education (in percentage of the corresponding age group) between Japan and Europe was 90 percent, in Japan's favor. An example will illustrate the effects of this situation. In 1850, China's silk industry was very advanced compared to Japan's. But when the silkworm illness struck, Japan appropriated Louis Pasteur's methods and eventually surpassed China, which was incapable of the same adjustments.

Deprived of engineers, poor countries must depend entirely on the outside world to borrow and adapt modern techniques. Thus, it is inevitable that, at one point or another along the chain, the process stops. The idea that foreign techniques can be imported purely and simply without at least partially adapting them to local conditions is naive. There is always a particular factor, such as the climate, that demands adaptation to local conditions. The progress of agriculture illustrates this essential idea. European countries became very innovative in agricultural matters between the seventeenth and the eighteenth centuries, with the Netherlands in the lead. This "agricultural revolution," as it was called, took place in a temperate climate. The availability of a high-yield strain of wheat that was more resistant to spring frosts evidently had no effect upon economies based on rice or those where the climate was different. From the start other innovations were necessary to adapt this variety to local conditions. The Canadian province of Manitoba did not become a major wheat-producing region until the beginning of the twentieth century. It had to wait for the availability of a quick-maturing new variety of wheat adapted to its particular climate, and this development was a result of intensive work by Canadian researchers. For a poor country that lacks the means to research innovations suitable to its needs, such an endeavor is impossible.[11]

Nineteenth-century France is also a good model to compare against India or China during this same period. After the Napoleonic wars, France was a backward country from an industrial viewpoint. Labor was cheap, a situation which allowed it to compensate for the lack of modern techniques but was hardly favorable to innovation. Internal demand was weak, which deprived French industries of attractive domestic outlets for their products. All the ingredients of a vicious circle of poverty were joined. However, between the fall of the first Napoleonic empire and the advent of the second—less than 50 years—the landscape changed completely. In 1851, at London's Crystal Palace Exhibition, French manufacturers displayed their industrial strength by exhibiting their new turbine engines, daguerreotypes, and textile dyes. In less than half a century, France evolved from being primarily an artisan economy whose sole comparative advantage was producing luxury goods. France was able to become rich by choosing a narrow path that consisted of imitating *and* innovating. The example of the regional development around Marseille was recently studied.[12]

Businesses first drew from the supply of workers released from crafts industries. Then the craftsmen quickly acquired the knowledge and competency necessary to innovate and set up machinery adapted to local needs. And so Marseille became leader in olive oil production and sugar refining. This is an example of production techniques that did not require specialized scientific expertise, such as the case of the steam engine during the period 1870–1890. The problem was different for steamships and locomotives. Between 1835 and 1845, more than 15 engineers and dozens of qualified British workers came to Marseille. The entire Mediterranean region experienced the same thing as Mohamed Ali's Egypt, Barcelona, and the kingdom of Two Sicilies of Ferdinand II. But in Marseille, in contrast with what happened in Egypt, the encounter of two "dynamics" helped these competencies take hold. "When technological innovation is not imposed, when it is anticipated during the course of a growth phase, then it can succeed."[13]

If no country can rely solely on international trade to prosper, it is also illusory to hope it can catch up to rich countries by remaining independent. In this regard the Asian development model is a textbook case. By encouraging exports, trade permits countries to dispose of foreign currency. That, in turn, furnishes it with the means to import scarce merchandise, notably manufacturing equipment that will aid economic growth. Here trade is a direct factor of growth. However, as in Japan after the Meiji Revolution, world trade is also a factor that very efficiently selects national champions; it is an element of a country's industrial policy. Foreign trade is one of the policy tools responsible for Asia's success.

Two opposing articles—one by Jeffrey Sachs and Andrew Warner, the other by Francisco Rodríguez and Dani Rodrik[14]—offer conflicting evidence about how to interpret the influence international trade has on economic growth. Sachs and Warner defined a group of "open" countries according to certain criteria, including the exchange rate regime and trade barriers. They showed that those nations belonging to the "open" group always experienced greater growth than those countries classified as "closed." During the period 1970–1995, the "open" economies grew at an average rate of 4.5 percent per year, whereas the "closed" economies' GDP only grew an average of 0.7 percent a year. Among the open economies, the growth rate of emerging economies was two percent faster than those of rich economies. In the closed economies, there was no difference. Trade openness thus seems propitious to for the "convergence" of poor and rich countries. According to Sachs and Warner, the result is in fact radical: with no exceptions countries that chose an "open" trade policy grew faster each year than closed countries. Those nations that changed strategies midway always experienced lower growth during the closed period than during the open period. Other studies refined these results. For example, Jeffrey Frankel and David Romer showed that geographic variables like access to the sea or proximity to large commercial centers are factors that contribute favorably to a country's economic growth.[15] In other words, each time that a nation finds itself in a situation where trade is easier to conduct, economic growth is stronger.

These conclusions were criticized by Rodríguez and Rodrik on the ground that they do not permit to distinguish the result of a favorable role for trade in the strict sense of this term from other related factors, such as good governance.[16] Regarding Sachs and Warner's interpretation that a proximity to commercial centers is propitious to trade, Rodríguez and Rodrik emphasize a fact that is in itself difficult to contest—neighboring nations influence a country in many other ways than just commercial exchanges. Rudiger Dornbusch emphasized this in his comments on the Sachs-Warner paper: ". . . merchandise trade is only a marginally important part of the openness that provides these benefits."[17] It is true that Sachs and Warner are not very explicit in identifying the mechanisms by which trade is a factor of growth. In his earlier works, Rodrik emphasized that economies which have a high export rate can afford to acquire equipment wares abroad that will stimulate their economic growth. In his more recent studies, Rodrik shows that open economies have more impact on a country's "institutions." An open society offers less incentives for nepotism or corruption than does a closed society. Other works confirm the narrow connection that exists between openness and the economic efficiency of institutions. Education offers a striking example of this. Pakistan offers a reminder that it is not sufficient merely to send children to school to be assured that they are "educated" in a sense conducive to economic growth. It is possible to prove that open societies generally make better use of educational instruction than closed societies do. The role of trade, we have seen, is both indirect and essential—it obligates open societies to make their domestic institutions effective.

This debate may well appear academic. Among the authors cited above, no one disagrees that "open" societies grow faster than the "closed" ones. This is emphasized by Rodríguez and Rodrik themselves: "We know of no credible evidence . . . that suggests trade restrictions are systematically associated with higher growth rates."[18] And indeed, since 1991 when it chose to open up to international trade, India (to revisit this emblematic example) experienced a growth rate higher than 6 percent a year, significantly higher than the annual rate it previously recorded. China does still better, with a figure that at times approached 10 percent a year. The rest of Asia is not far behind. Despite its 1997 financial crisis, growth in this region averaged more than 5 percent per year throughout the 1990s. Whatever the exact means are, the facts are unequivocal. Asian countries, with no less than 60 percent of the world's population, have apparently discovered a new method, composed of trade openness and internal investments, whose principal merit is to factually contradict the seemingly inexorable idea that "wealth always goes to wealth."

The Levers of Riches

Today the world's population consists of 1 billion rich people, 2.5 billion poor people, and 2.5 billion very poor people. In current dollars, taken together the poor and the very poor countries represent only 20 percent of the world's wealth, distributed among 85 percent of the total population. With regard to the poorest nations, the figure is even more startling—these account for only 3 percent of the world's wealth, but account for 40 percent of the planet's inhabitants. Economists have remarked that these figures exaggerate the poverty of the very poorest nations. Life is by definition cheaper in a poor country—it costs less to house and to care for oneself. Yet a billion people are still living entirely on the equivalent of $1 a day[19]—less than what one spends having an espresso on the terrace of a Parisian café or buying a daily newspaper.[20]

Analyzing under-development in 1969, Arghiri Emmanuel concluded that poor countries were necessarily exploited by rich nations. His rationale partly depended on the fact that the only supposed source of wealth was, in his view, human labor. If one hour of labor in Bombay is paid less than an hour in Detroit, it is inevitable that the American worker is exploiting the Indian laborer. Today it is no longer possible to understand wealth by making such a comparison—infrastructure, telephones, electricity, and computers are also factors that must be taken into account. A study conducted by the International Federation of Textile Industries illustrates this by comparing the performances of the textile industries in a number of countries. In the comparison between India and the United States, in the interval of a century, we recognize the comparison that Gregory Clark proposed.[21]

First of all, the number of working hours needed to manufacture a given piece of cloth does not vary significantly from one country to another. It is barely 8 percent higher in India than in the United States; the role of work rhythms and organizational efficiency is not dominant. We are far from the considerable differences that Clark recorded in the nineteenth century. The ratio between the cost of salaries in these two countries is unfathomable: an hour of work costs 1/15 as much in India as in the United States. With respect to these figures, one would expect that the Indian cloth would be much cheaper. But this is not the case. Except for labor, all the other cost factors are higher in India.[22] Energy, for example, is twice as expensive, and capital costs 50 percent more than raw materials. Even raw cotton (partly due to U.S. subsidies to its cotton producers) is more costly in India. What seems *a priori* an exceptional advantage—low labor costs—is diluted in a very unfavorable global cost structure when the costs of capital and energy are taken into account. In fact, in the present study under consideration, only the textile industries in Brazil and South Korea have lower manufacturing costs than the United States.

The Theory of Levers

The wealth of a nation is furthered by the operation of a series of levers that raise one another—they are not driven by human labor alone. A primary lever is the one operated by education or professional experience, what economists call human capital. A person who knows how to read and write will be more capable than someone who is illiterate. The second lever is what is offered by machines, the physical capital that a worker operates. An engineer will not have the same efficiency if he or she does not have a computer. Machines themselves enact a third, more mysterious lever called "global efficiency," which includes technological progress and the organizational efficiency of businesses. Bugs in computers, like those in a good labor organization, gear down the efficiency of human and physical capital. These three dimensions explain modern economic growth and help to illuminate the causes of poverty in poor countries.

The same levers operate in poor countries as in wealthy ones. The drama is that in poor nations each of these levers are slightly staggered compared to what is found in the rich countries.[23] Soto and I calculate that poor countries suffer from a 35 percent handicap in each of these three factors. When a worker in a wealthy country operates a lever whose corresponding value is 100, his counterpart in a poor country controls a lever whose corresponding average value is only 65. Human and physical capital and global efficiency are each about one-third lower. A worker in a poor country has at his disposal only 65 percent of the total capacity of one level, multiplied by 65 percent and re-multiplied by 65 percent, which finally yields only 27 percent of the resources available in the rich countries, which explains why the ratio of income between rich countries and poor ones is about 4:1. The result is even more spectacular for countries at the bottom of the scale. For example, in Africa each of the three components of wealth possess about half the levels found in the wealthiest nations. After we progressively multiply each of these three terms, an African worker is no more than 12.5 percent as productive as a worker in a rich country. Thus, we are far removed from Gregory Clark's explanation, which, in the framework of Indian textile factories in the nineteenth century, brought everything back to labor productivity. Production is much more complex than it was in the past. A poor nation can no longer hope to catch up to rich countries by content-ing itself merely with accelerating the work rate, even if it succeeds at that goal. Low labor costs do not compen-sate, or only do so with difficulty, for the global handi-caps of an impoverished society: weak infrastructure (expensive energy), higher prices for raw materials (which is in itself absurd), and higher capital costs due to global scarcity.

It is the fact that these handicaps are cumulative that today makes it extremely difficult to escape poverty. Neither education nor investment nor the purchase of foreign technology is sufficient if not used in conjunction with the other levers of growth. Capital perfectly illus-trates the vicious cycle. On average, a laborer in a poor country uses 1/5 as much capital as a worker engaging in the same task in a rich country. Far from making capital flow to the country where it is scarce, financial global-ization is very parsimonious with respect to poor coun-tries. This phenomenon, known as Lucas's Paradox, has provoked innumerable controversies among economists. Why does capitalism not supply workers in poor coun-tries with the machinery that would make them produc-tive? The answer has to do with the fact that it could be efficient to add physical capital to the poor countries from a technical point of view, but that this is not necessarily the case from a financial perspective. In New York it could be perfectly profitable financially to computerize a grocery store, a school, or a hospital, but in Lagos customers are too poor to pay the prices necessitated by the presence of such equipment. Nothing can be bought on the global market with the equivalent earnings of $1 a day, even if one enjoys a greater purchasing power due to living among other people who earn so little. Poverty here is a vicious, cumulative circle.

Yet by confronting each of the growth-hindering handicaps (people's education, imported machinery, technology) one by one, a country can, in theory, get out of poverty. But the sacrifices to accomplish this are immense, if it wants to confront them at the same time. By itself financial globalization is unable to create the conditions that will make a society globally productive. Inversely, we can understand why the "tense" strategies of the Asian countries that simultaneously engaged the three levers of growth proved so effective.

Development as Freedom

Lee Kwan Yew, the leader of Singapore, championed Asian authoritarianism, explaining among other things that the prohibition against chewing gum was a component of Asian growth.[24] This idea that the Asian model, scorning the individualist and libertarian values of the West, is both more efficient and the only way to oppose these values, was often theorized, but always by the regime in power. Amartya Sen offered the best critique of this vision in his book *Development as Freedom*: "Aung San Suu Kyi has no less legitimacy—indeed clearly has rather more—in interpreting what the Burmese want than have the military rulers of Myanmar, whose candidates she had defeated in open elections before being put in jail by the defeated military junta."[25] To think of freedom as a Western attribute is to engage in the unfortunate habit of judging the past in light of the present, to forget the Inquisition and the tragedies of the twentieth century.

Not only has it not been proven that gross domestic product (GDP) is higher in dictatorships (even if the analysis in limited to developing countries), but the idea is a contradiction in terms. For Sen, "the ends and means of development call for placing the perspective of freedom at the center of the stage. The people have to be seen, in this perspective, as being actively involved—given the opportunity—in shaping their own destiny, and not just as passive recipients of the fruits of cunning development programs."[26] Sen apprehends the objective of economic development as "the valuation of the actual freedoms enjoyed by the people involved."[27] Free access to education and health care are constitutive elements of development. While these are means to an end, education and health care are above all ends in themselves.

For an economist, a nation's gross domestic product is the alpha and the omega of economic development. But

Sen invites us to be suspicious of the reasoning that a rich person can supply himself with all he wants, including leisure, and then he is free. Material wealth is indisputably an element of human freedom. A world of deprivation is not a world where one can live in conformity with one's expectations. But the perspective of freedom sensibly alters the link that can be established between economic development and development. According to economic reasoning, a person who is given the choice between carrots and cauliflower and opts for the carrots does not need someone to offer him the cauliflower in order to be happy. The ability to make a choice, nevertheless, is itself an essential step of human liberty. To bring development back to its consequences, ignoring the process that leads it there, is reductive. This makes Sen extremely severe with respect to the idea that authoritarian regimes—such as that of Lee Kwan Yew—could be proponents of development.

A comparison between India and China is illuminating here. It is sometimes said that India suffers from being a democracy and that this is one of the reasons why it has experienced slower growth than China. For Sen, the explanation is much more direct. It is a fact that India still has an abnormally high proportion of illiterates (more than 50 percent of its population). The percentage of illiterates is less than half as great in China. Elitism and the caste system drove India to privilege the education of the elites, which explains, moreover, why Bangalore (India's high-technology city) posted such good results. Public policy in matters of health and education constituted a veritable denial of freedom for the majority of people. When India instituted an active commercial policy in 1991, poor education of the vast majority of the population explained why it was much less well-equipped to capitalize on this open policy than China.

Despite their poverty, Costa Rica and the Indian state of Kerala obtained excellent results in education and in access to health care. As with Cuba, however, these results did not give rise to economic growth. In both cases, economic policies hostile to private investment and to the development of markets canceled the benefits produced by improving human capital. As in Ghana, which bet everything on the sole accumulation of physical capital, growth was interrupted in Kerala because it wagered everything on the sole accumulation of human capital. Sen extends this logic and treats the denial of the market itself as a similar denial of freedom. Thus, the passage from servile labor to free labor, whatever the ups and downs of the latter, is a sign of development. This does not negate the need to correct the market's perverse effects by redistributive policies for instance. Moreover, Sen is ferocious with respect to European countries that, by allowing mass unemployment, separated a considerable number of individuals from this dimension of freedom—the ability to work if they want. But if today servile labor is a faraway image in "developed" nations, in many poor countries it remains a tragic dimension of the human condition, from child labor to the exploitation of women.

The idea that development must be interpreted as the search for the freedom to be and act according to one's aspirations makes it possible to clarify what constitutes inequality. It is not the same thing to be poor in a rich country as to be poor in a poor country. Sen's perspective enables us to understand why. The poor in a rich country are quite often wealthier, from a material point of view, than the poor in a poor country. If the poor in a rich country suffer from social exclusion, the relative poverty that holds them apart from the goods to which the other inhabitants have access, this deprives them of an essential dimension of human life: interacting with others. To be illiterate in a population in which everyone else knows how to read is to lose a crucial dimension of the capacity that shapes happiness: acting in concert with others and participating in the elaboration of a public decision.

The link between inequality and participation in the public sphere is rich with implications. The most egalitarian societies are also those that have produced the highest levels of education and the best health outcomes. A famous study by Samuel Preston shows that England registered a significant increase in life expectancy over the course of two periods, 1911–1921 and 1940–1951, in which world wars occurred.[28] Whereas earlier or later episodes in English history recorded an increase in life expectancy that varied between 1 year and 4 years, depending on the period, these two wartime periods saw an increase of more than $6\frac{1}{2}$ years. How was this possible? Quite simply because the two wars favored an accelerated democratization of the health system and greater access to basic nourishment. It was during the World War II, for example, that the rate of malnutrition collapsed in Great Britain. Waging war creates a social demand for equality, which proves propitious for the provision of shared public goods.

Another example illustrates the depth of this idea. Comparing the Philippines and South Korea at the beginning of the 1960s, Robert Lucas, a winner of the Nobel Prize in economics and one of the founders of the "endogenous growth" theory, underscored that these two countries displayed the same global characteristics—the same levels of education, urbanization, and per-capita income. Trying to understand why South Korea later experienced exceptional growth while the Philippines registered much less growth, Lucas explained that it was necessary to believe in "miracles." South Korea's miracle was that it believed in its chances; the Philippines did not. Picking up on this example, Roland Bénabou showed that an essential dimension ignored by Lucas accounted for the difference between South Korea and the Philippines.[29] The Philippines had a higher level of inequality than Latin American countries. Soon after Japan's defeat and the re-nationalization of occupied lands, South Korea engaged in agricultural reform. By doing so, it considerably reduced its inequality. For Bénabou, this lower inequality is one of the conditions that favor the establishment of an effective educational system. Whereas in Latin America the elites send their children abroad to study, and in India the caste system perpetuates a very unequal access to education, South Korea inherited (or endowed itself with after World War II) a sufficiently egalitarian society so that the idea of mass education quickly became a fundamental principle there. Since then, the virtuous circle of "endogenous growth" has come into play. Today, South Korea spends as high a percentage of its GDP on education and research as rich countries do.

Sen's theories, interpreting development as a quest for freedom, will not reassure those who are worried by the hegemonic temptations of "new" regional powers, such as China and India. The political and geopolitical effects of Chinese or Indian growth are wide open. Conflicts can just as well emerge today in Asia as in Europe at the dawn of the twentieth century. A lower birth rate does not suffice to show that women have won the battle for their emancipation. Similarly, a country's rapid economic growth does not by itself demonstrate that the forces of freedom have won. However, nothing would be more naive than to think that China's growth is only an instrument of the willpower its leadership. Economic development nourishes new aspirations, just as it feeds on them. It opens new possibilities without ascribing them to a preordained agenda. The determination of those who see the march of human history toward a peaceful end is, in this regard, certainly naive, but no more so than the mechanical vision of those who obstinately believe that the conflict between civilizations is fixed in the form of an immutable past.

6

The Empire, Etcetera

The American Superpower Reflected in Europe's Mirror

The rejection of globalization in France is often conflated with a distrust of the United States as a superpower. The contemporary United States is said to combine the hegemony of yesterday's imperial powers with today's world economy. According to its detractors, its influence is universal in its effects and selfish in its motivation. However, in *The Rise and Fall of the Great Powers*, a book that enjoyed great success in 1987, the British historian Paul Kennedy (then a professor at Yale University) argued that the United States was descending from its high pedestal and yielding its prominence to Japan. Kennedy announced a thesis of "Imperial Overstretch" and predicted the decline of the United States.[1] Every great power, he explained, eventually dissipates its strength until it is ruined. A public finance crisis sounded the death knell of the Roman Empire, the Spanish Empire, and later the British Empire, and a similar situation at the end of the twentieth century was threatening to end the dominance of the United States. In the mid 1980s, Kennedy's contention was supported by the Reagan administration's monumental public deficit, which Kennedy interpreted as announcing the start of the decline of the United States. That history's great empires have almost always been doomed by public finance crises is an indisputable fact already demonstrated by numerous economic historians.[2] However, what had been true for a long time is no longer true today. In the age of income taxes and value-added taxes, the nature of the fiscal question has changed. One (tough) decision made at the beginning of Bill Clinton's first term stopped the Reagan-era deficit spending and put America's economic growth back on track. Immediately after taking office, George W. Bush's administration renewed the cycle of deficits, using a well-tried conservative technique for privatizing the state known as "starving the beast" (meaning that if public finances are not available then certain public expenditures cannot be made). The expenses of the Department of Defense, the heart of the empire, however, were hardly threatened by these political tactics.

In fact, a fundamental difference between the imperial powers of yesterday and the United States today makes any comparison largely superficial. An empire's natural propensity is to rely on the wealth of its colonies in order to prosper. This was notably the case in the Roman Empire and also, up to a certain point, the British Empire. The Romans quickly mobilized the Empire's resources to Rome's own benefit. Egypt and Gaul were responsible for supplying Rome with wheat; the Middle East supplied textiles; amphorae came from Greece; metals came from Spain.[3] Not that the Romans lacked their own inventive spirit. In 100 B.C., Rome was better equipped with paved roads, sewers, and food and water than were most European capitals in 1800. The Romans showed exceptional ingenuity in architecture and in road construction. They inherited tools perfected by the Greeks—the lever, the screw, the pulley, the cog wheel—that allowed them to make military equipment, but whose civilian uses remained untapped for centuries. Strictly speaking, economic life was indeed poor between 500 B.C. and 500 A.D. In the agricultural domain, Europe lagged behind the great irrigation projects that were undertaken in Egypt and Mesopotamia. In the industrial sector during ancient times and the Middle Ages, Europe remained far behind China's accomplishments. According to the economic historian Joel Mokyr,[4] ancient Greco-Roman society was never very creative from a strictly technical viewpoint. They constructed aqueducts but did not really utilize hydraulic power. They mastered glass manufacturing and understood how to use solar power, but they did not invent eyeglasses. While the economy was (already) driven by private enterprise, the Roman Empire engaged in little innovative activity.

Using a distinction proposed by Mokyr, two types of economic growth can be identified: that which is motivated by a "Smithian" logic, following Adam Smith's vision expressed in *The Wealth of Nations*, and that which responds to a Schumpeterian logic (named for the economist Joseph Schumpeter). Adam Smith said that a big market favored an efficient division of labor between people; today, one would also say between different regions in the same economy. This division of labor is a source of prosperity, particularly, as we just saw, for empires. Schumpeterian logic says that growth depends on the innovative capacity of an economy. In theory, nothing prevents combining the benefits of these two types of growth. Nevertheless, trying to optimize resource usage over the largest possible territory is not the same as trying to innovate in a given market.

The Schumpeterian cycle of innovation truly began in Europe during the Middle Ages. Europe abandoned making amusing gadgets and Greco-Roman weapons and gradually began producing innovations that aimed to reduce the harshness of ordinary life and to improve the material life of the masses. Medieval Europe was perhaps the first society to build an economic system that tried to save human labor—the sweat of slaves and coolies. A fair number of misconceptions about the nature of capitalism originate here. The horse, which Jared Diamond showed to have had a decisive role in ancient society, only became productive from a strictly economic viewpoint during the Middle Ages. The harness collar was perfected then, allowing horses to be made into work animals; previously the belt threatened to strangle them if they had to pull a load that was too heavy. The entire history of Europe from the Middle Ages to the present day is characterized by a new kind of economic growth in which technological innovation is endless. Whereas "Smithian" growth necessarily ends by exhausting itself, Schumpeterian growth is *a priori* without limit. Each bottleneck or impediment gives rise to an innovation that solves the problem. The first misunderstanding regarding American power in the contemporary world comes into play here. The United States may be an imperial power in the political sense of the term, but it is barely such a power, or not one at all, in the economic sense. It is foremost a Schumpeterian economy.

The Decline of Europe?
Today Europe seems to have changed direction and seems to be carried more by a Smithian logic than a Schumpeterian one. The large European common market favors rationalizing and reorganizing tasks on a continental scale.[5] Schumpeterian growth is brought about by a constantly evolving technology—to grow, a firm takes

the place of a rival by offering a more innovative product. For a long time, innovation was the engine of Europe's economic growth. Now it is the engine of economic growth in the United States, where patent applications in the high-technology sector are twice as numerous as in Europe. New companies are not, strictly speaking, more numerous in the United States than in Europe; they are more innovative, and five years after their creation American companies experience much stronger growth than their European counterparts. Europe has few international champions comparable to Microsoft, Intel, Cisco Systems, IBM, Dell, and Compaq. Although Europe has some strength in cellular phone technology, it is necessary to keep in mind that the research departments of a number of Europe's "champions," such as Finland's Nokia, are in the United States. In the case of mobile telephones, Europe profits from a "Smithian" advantage: a common standard throughout its geographic territory. In the *Business Week* rankings, Europe has six of the top 100 firms in the new economy; the US has 75.

It is sometimes said that Europe has a less innovative culture than the United States; however, the history of the nineteenth century and beginning of the twentieth century invalidates this idea. Europe was Schumpeterian in the nineteenth century, when the United States was Smithian and was preoccupied with the creation of a domestic market. There were a number of factors in the changing of these roles, among them World War II. It is possible that Europe henceforth found its comparative advantage in the current situation: to remain slightly behind the United States in technological matters, and to make good choices after the fact. Paul Geroski, an American economist who emigrated to England, recalls being astonished by European color television: though it was a decade behind the United States, Europe had made a superior technological choice. Yet what appeared as a shrewd strategy to Geroski was viewed in Europe as a result more passively submitted to than desired.

Innovation is the nerve center of the New Economy. For the new information or pharmaceutical technologies, it has become almost the exclusive object of economic activity. With regard to overall statistics, the larger European countries do not seem behind in research and development, but Europe as a whole spends much less on research and development than the United States. If the data presented by Ugur Muldur complementing a report by Élie Cohen and Jean-Hervé Lorenzi for the Conseil d'Analyse Economique[6] are to be believed, the cumulative difference in expenditures on R&D by the 15 European Union member states relative to the United States between 1990 and 1997 amounted to $386 billion.[7] In recent years Europe has a deficit of about $60 billion annually on high-technology research relative to the United States. European research remains furthermore a compilation of national research agendas, the total of which is worth less than the sum of its individual components. The procedures by which the European Union allocates community resources are very careful to respect the equality between nations; this is one of the reasons why the EU has not succeeded in fostering the development of high-tech clusters in Europe, whereas in the United States research centers are concentrated near the great universities. Few Europeans would accept clustering resources near Oxford or Bologna as they are clustered around Boston or San Francisco, if only because of the difficulties cause by different languages. The role played by the Department of Defense in the United States is hardly transferable to the European situation. Whereas American R&D profits from the effects of agglomeration, Europe has not managed to find a formula that lends itself to its history and its geography.

Europe has been "behind" the United States for many years. The "thirty glorious years" (as they are called in France) after World War II were one of the most famous episodes in which Europe managed to catch up. The management methods that French industries had copied from the United States were not far from those that already existed in Europe. Both drew from the same source: the industrial revolution that occurred at the start of the twentieth century, to which France and Germany contributed strongly. We also cannot disregard the desire to forget the war and proceed with reconstruction. The

French automobile firm Renault (whose owner was tried for acts of collaboration with the Nazis) is emblematic of this desire. The current situation is different. The fact that today virtually all new technology comes from the United States creates a painful sentiment of dispossession. In *The Clash of Civilizations*, Samuel Huntington, invoking Carroll Quigley, wrote that a civilization declines as soon as it stops innovating.[8] The problem that the United States poses to the world stems from the fact that innovation has become its comparative advantage. The percentage of Americans who major in engineering is in steady decline, but the US has no difficulty replacing them with Indians or Europeans, who are well rewarded. For India and China, the exchange is not unequal. The Chinese learned a long time ago to profit from the advantages of their diaspora. Their income differential with the United States is so stratospheric that they undoubtedly experience the same elation at trying to catch up to the US that the Europeans experienced during their "thirty glorious years."

For Europeans, who were "in contact" with the United States during most of the twentieth century, the medicine is more bitter. Will Europeans react? Probably, but not certainly. Joel Mokyr attributes England's decline in the nineteenth century to its failure to create engineering schools like those founded in France and Germany during this period, which would have allowed the children and grandchildren of the inventors of the steam engine and the loom to continue their parents' innovations. Nevertheless, according to Mokyr, the worthy offspring of these innovative geniuses attended English "public" (private) schools but left England at the dawn of the twentieth century. None of the great inventions that would shape the twentieth century (e.g., the internal-combustion engine, or the electric motor) originated in England. Beyond the European case and beyond all considerations of economic efficiency, the world cannot be "fair" if all peoples do not feel they are contributing to the increase of knowledge that shapes it.

Europe, School of Globalization

The United States is at once a producer of sneakers, medicines, movies, software, and immaterial goods for the world's use and a large but "provincial" domestic economy. The European economic model is different. Europe, formidably diverse culturally and historically, is unable to surmount the obstacles to political integration. The European model is a source of inspiration for Asian countries that do not intend to be absorbed by China and for Latin American countries that have similar fears about the United States. It is a good model whose only inconvenience is that it is not as universal as the Europeans would like.

Despite its failures and partly because of them, Europe does offer several lessons about "globalization." The

European Union has, above all, always succeeded at reabsorbing the income inequalities between its member nations. Ireland, which began far behind the other continental countries, is today among the EU's wealthiest nations. At a slower but still significant rate, Spain, Portugal, and Greece are catching up to the European average income. Is this convergence caused by the European common market, European common institutions, or regional aid funds? This question is certainly important for the experts, and it will count even more as the European Union adds ten new member states. But with respect to the historical result, it has little importance. Once integrated into a group having Europe's institutional coherence, the poor countries will converge toward the living standards of the rich countries.

Europe is sometimes reproached for being a vector of globalization by submitting the individual European economies to the same rules of the global market. It is an unjust accusation if judged by the national income convergences Europe has produced. However, Europe has succumbed to the same paradoxical effects of globalization. The decline in the cost of distance did not protect regions from the effects of "agglomeration." Although the reduction in differences between nations has not waned, regional inequalities stopped diminishing more than 20 years ago. In France, the Parisian megalopoly, the so-called Île-de-France region, alone produces 40 percent of the nation's GDP, a domination that has hardly been menaced by the availability of the Internet or high-speed trains. The Île-de-France region does not suffer from globalization. Yet, the loss of jobs there is no less than in France's other regions. But the creation of jobs in the Île-de-France is also very lively. In regions that are still holdovers of an industrial specialization inherited from the nineteenth century, so far as globalization encourages passage toward a post-industrial society, it exacts a considerable human cost. It is in this sense that Europe is sometimes interpreted as the conductor of globalization.

Europe offers one important lesson. It shows that economic integration does not at all entail the eradication of cultural diversity. In view of the diversity of the Swedes, the Italians, the Germans, and the French, or even the Portuguese and the Spanish, one should not fear that an integrated global market erases the world's plurality. For those who are keen to maintain cultural diversity between people, it is possible to say that Europe sharpens these distinctions more than it eliminates them. Catalans and Corsicans have demanded greater autonomy, knowing they are protected economically by Europe and the euro. The economic efficiency argument which maintains it is necessary to be a large nation (in the demographic sense of the term) in order to be prosperous no longer holds water. In fact, the six wealthiest European countries are the six smallest: Luxembourg, the

Netherlands, the three Scandinavian countries, and Ireland. At work here is the mechanism Bénabou described: Egalitarian societies can set faster growth in motion. The foundation of what could be called Europe's success—to achieve economic integration that is also respectful of cultural diversity—is also emblematic of its incapacity to create a whole nation-state. It is because Europe strives for this cultural and economic objective that, for the moment, it has failed to attain its political objective.

The World Order[9]

After the terrorist attacks of September 11, 2001, the Bush administration immediately negotiated with the pharmaceutical industry for unrestricted use of Cipro, the medical antidote for anthrax; it also indemnified the industries affected by the attack (aviation, insurance, tourism) and enacted an additional lowering of interest rates. No effort seems to have been spared to enable the US economy to emerge from the crisis rapidly. Europe's reaction was quite different; it appeared as a giant prisoner of rules and procedures. The European states had to engage in delicate negotiations in order to obtain authorization to offer subsidies to the sectors affected by the crisis. The budgetary response was framed by the stability pact; and after much delay, the European Central Bank ended up agreeing to lower interest rates but on the condition that pressure directed against it stop. A frank report published by Notre Europe (a foundation presided over by Jacques Delors) contains this sentence: "While in the United States an informal meeting between the Federal Reserve's chairman and the Treasury Secretary is sufficient for a constructive exchange of views, all dialogue in the euro zone must inevitably involve a lot more people."[10]

As Élie Cohen and Jean Pisani-Ferry noted, in Europe everything is done so that no one ever has to make a real decision.[11] Everything must follow rules agreed to previously. The European Central Bank and the Stability and Growth Pact are perfect examples of this attitude. In "specialized" fields, such as competition policy and sanitary norms, Europe can create effective and credible supranational regulation. But Europe is incapable of adapting to particular circumstances. All normally constituted governments know, for example, that they have to give aid to victims of an unforeseeable disaster. The essential task of government is to use its discretionary power when the rules are not adaptable or are simply absent. The English philosopher John Locke said that the proper use of executive power is to resolve cases for which rules are not yet expressed. As the theorist of exceptional conditions Carl Schmitt remarked, wars can only be conducted by sovereign states, precisely because war involves a domain where the exception is the rule. A normally constituted government is credited with legitimacy, more than it possesses an absolute legitimacy, which allows it to deal with unforeseen circumstances, like a household facing exceptional expenses—the government's credibility is renewed at each election. Deprived of this elective moment, agencies such as the European Commission can only function from given rules. These agencies will never possess the moment of radical liberty given to a normally constituted executive in the face of exceptional circumstances.

At the opening of the convention charged with drafting a European constitution, President Valéry Giscard d'Estaing of France, who was chairing the convention, perfectly explained the difficulty of the exercise with respect to what would be involved in writing and editing an ordinary democratic constitution. Europe, he explained, is composed of people *and* states. This is a fundamental idea, quickly forgotten by those for whom the state is merely an instrument at the disposal of the people. States have an autonomous existence, to which the people are attached. The first idea that came to the minds of philosophers and politicians is that states are the legitimate actors in world affairs. The United Nations was thought of as a new agora of the world. However, the way the Iraq war was handled immediately shows the limits of this analogy. In a representative democracy, all citizens are considered equal. Even if it is an operative fiction, it is a creative fiction, an idea in whose name people are ready to fight. In the case of international relations, this fiction does not work. First of all, states vary in size of population. This point seems minor, but it is not. Were Europe made up of five or six states the size of France, a good number of the institutional difficulties (such as the rotation of presidents and the relative weight of small countries in the European Commission) would be resolved immediately. But Luxembourg will never have the same rank as France or Germany. The idea of a global democracy founded on all states' being equal cannot function, except very metaphorically.

To this problem of the heterogeneity of size is obviously added to the heterogeneity of wealth. Rich countries cannot run the risk of giving poor countries the least claim on their wealth. Purse strings are not shared.

An Economic Council

In order to correct for its incapacity to adhere to the simple duality of ordinary representative democracies founded on the government-parliament pairing, Europe had to add a third element to its institutional edifice: the European Commission. Based on the idea that one day it would form Europe's government, it has remained a thorn in the side to sovereignists (who challenge its authority) and to federalists (who rail against its weakness). The trio of European Commission, European

Counsel, and European Parliament illustrates, however, an essential institutional innovation. The Counsel, which represents the individual European states, has the last word, and the Parliament, which represents the people, is endowed with deliberative power. Meanwhile, the task of articulating the first word of defining an agenda is charged to the European Commission, which is the guardian of the "European public good." From a political point of view, the European model offers a solution to the problem of global "governance" when there is no world government.

The simple fact of being able to set an agenda turns out to have considerable effective power. It allows the Commission from the outset to discard any choices that are incompatible with the "European project." It would never propose, for example, that one country should be taxed in order to finance the needs of all the others even if, assuming it was put to a vote, such a proposition would delight the other countries. The philosopher John Rawls said that a measure is just if it can be approved by people kept in ignorance of whom it benefits. If Paul does not know that he will be told to take care of Peter, Paul will admit that he who is hungry should be fed by him who is full. To call a European agenda "just" consists of making propositions that would be acceptable regardless of what European nationality is the ultimate beneficiary. Thus, the role of the European Commission consists of taking the place of the European citizen in that citizen's absence. It is this creative fiction that provides an understanding of the strengths and the limits of the European model. It offers an institutional solution to the quest of a public good while falling short of a true democracy. This is exactly the problem to which the world at large needs to find a solution.

AIDS and Debt

"The Sick Are in the South ..."

"The sick are in the South, and the medicines are in the North." These words are from Bernard Kouchner, one of the founders of Doctors without Borders, the humanitarian organization awarded the 1999 Nobel Peace Prize. Several million people die in Africa every year, because they lack access to medicines that nevertheless do exist. Here is a reminder of the abysmal figures associated with AIDS. Of the 34 million people infected around the world, 25 million live in Africa. In South Africa, estimates are 4 million people, or 20 percent of the country's adult population. In Botswana, 36 percent of the adult population is affected, and life expectancy barely exceeds 29 years. The cycle is hellish: young girls are contaminated by adult men, and children are infected by their mothers at birth or through nursing. Worse still, when preventive medicines are used (during pregnancy, for example) these are used in an insufficient manner, creating a resistance in the virus that makes later treatment even more problematic.

To die of a disease for which the remedy already exists is not like envying the owner of a pair of shoes that one would like to wear in his place. Not only is it unfair in the ordinary sense of the word; it is inefficient in the economic sense. There is an immense difference between intellectual property and property in general. To buy a house is to claim the legal right to use it. I wear my shoes; you don't, unless I lend them to you. The exclusive right associated with ownership of this type of property is embodied in the virtue of principles which hold that "the cobbler is master in his own house," and it caused property to figure into the "inalienable and sacred" rights of modern man. The nature of intellectual property is entirely different. A song or a chemical formula is neither bought nor consumed in the usual sense of the term that describes the use of physical goods. These are ideas and not objects; they survive the various private uses made of them. When an idea is discovered, nothing stops everyone from using it if not intellectual property rights, such as patents or copyright. Whereas physical property alone makes the appropriation of an object possible, intellectual-property laws restrict the free use of something that theoretically has no limits. Deprived of an owner, an ordinary good is not consumable. In the case of intellectual property, nothing of the sort takes place. An idea can be used by everyone without contradiction, and no-thing guarantees that a system in which all potential ideas would be protected by property rights would be efficient.

In principle, the best way to find a new idea with which to solve a given problem is to coordinate the research of those who work in the area and, once the discovery is made, to put the result at everyone's disposal. The reference model here is not the market but academic research, which compensates the researcher while leaving the discoveries free to all.[1] The intellectual-property system manages to do exactly the opposite. Competing teams researching the same topic (for example, a drug for a certain illness) do not share their knowledge, and once the discovery is achieved it will be the exclusive property of the one who first realized it. For the contemporary world, here is an extension of an idea articulated by Marx, a contradiction between productive forces (here, innovation) and property rights.

The question of genetically modified organisms (GMOs) offers another good example of what is at stake. José Bové, the French peasant who became famous for burning a McDonald's restaurant, noted in a letter to Mike Moore (the former Prime Minister of New Zealand who was then the director of the World Trade Organization) that the rural workers in the South are up to "a thousand times less productive" than the peasants in the North, by which he meant to imply that world trade could never be fair. In Africa, where sterile land has resisted the "green revolution" of the 1960s, complete self-sufficiency of the kind that Bové wants would in fact mean that the affected populations would continue to pay a lot for their food. The United Nations Development Program's 2002 report, recommended using GMOs in poor countries to break this impasse. If GMOs necessitate some precaution with respect to public health, they pose an even greater economic problem. Throughout history, the peasantry has been allowed to plant seeds freely. GMOs expose them to the risk of dependence on groups that will withhold the legal right to use them. Without "fair" regulation of intellectual property, conflicts can only escalate. Patents are essentially based on technical considerations. Unlike other authorities, such as those concerned with competition, patent agencies do not ask questions about social welfare. It is crucial that the cases involving competition convey a regulatory judgment, just as they ordinarily do in other cases where there is a risk of monopoly.

The "new economy's" cultural contradictions, as in the case of medicines, give rise to a much crueler moral contradiction. The global pharmaceutical market is very prosperous and flourishing. It should soon reach $4 trillion a year. More than 80 percent of this market is situated in the wealthy countries that are members of the Organization for Economic Cooperation and Development. This is why medicines are expensive: the rich are able and willing to pay for improving their health. Medicines are increasingly sophisticated and perform better, and their prices incorporate much higher R&D expenses, which in and of itself is perfectly normal. The problem does not lie there, however. It lies in the fact that in this global market poor countries have to pay just as much for their medicines as rich countries. A study written for the Macroeconomy and Health Commission, presided over by Jeffrey Sachs for the World Health Organization, established that, on average, poor countries pay for their medicines 85 percent of the price charged to wealthy countries. For 98 of the 465 drugs studied, the commission established that in practice prices are higher in poor countries. At these prices, the demand is practically zero. A generic drug, which would have the same medicinal properties but would not include the amortization of the pharmaceutical firms' investment costs in its selling price, may cost only one-tenth as much as the brand-name medicine. Why does the model of the "new economy," which permits worldwide distribution of movies if the admission price is adapted to the local market, not function in the one case where we would want it to?

The principle reason given by the pharmaceutical firms is they fear that generic medications may be illegally sold to poor countries and then exported back to the wealthy nations. Certainly there are a fair number of counterfeit items illegally introduced to the American market:

cigarettes, t-shirts, etc. Yet, as the British non-government organization Oxfam emphasizes, there is no sign that pharmaceutical products account for a significant amount of the products on this list. And it is not difficult to understand why. One can smoke contraband cigarettes or carry a counterfeit designer bag. To take unlabeled pills is much riskier. Furthermore, why should one take this risk, seeing that in most cases it is not the individual consumer who pays for the drug but the insurance companies or the welfare system? Therefore, the official argument does not hold water. The unacknowledged reason is found elsewhere. It is the political risk that generic products pose to the "legitimacy" of established prices in the rich countries. Pharmaceutical firms fear that it will become too difficult to justify selling a drug at $1,000 for a month's supply when a generic equivalent exists that costs only $50. It is to protect themselves from having to justify these high prices that they use dual pricing.

The collision of the new economy's economic inefficiencies and the "moral contradictions" that pit the rich against the poor, the question of medicines constitutes an explosive cocktail, which leaps at the figure of pharmaceutical industry. The president of a large pharmaceutical firm declared producing generic AIDS drugs an act of piracy likely to be eradicated as piracy was in the seventeenth century. Under pressure from public opinion, he had to retract that statement. Medicines are not the property of laboratories in the sense that they have the right to do with them as they wish. The sole fact of a medication's very existence morally obliges wealthy countries. Even though more elaboration of the details is needed, the right to manufacture and export generic drugs to poor countries was finally permitted by the World Trade Organization.

"Drop the Debt"

With the support of Pope John Paul II and the rock singer Bono, a formidable campaign for canceling the debt of poor countries was launched just before the end of the millennium. With biblical precepts resonating in the background, "Jubilee 2000" signaled the shift that can occur between people's moral convictions and the cold reasoning of economic calculations.

Debt cancellation has a long tradition. History abounds with circumstances where it changed the course of the world. According to some British historians, the French Revolution owes a great deal to the fact that France ruined itself by supporting the American colonies' war for independence against England, accumulating a debt that it was then unable to repay. Closer to our own era, John Maynard Keynes became famous just after World War I for the book *The Economic Consequences of the Peace*, in which he advises the victors "to make a bonfire" of Germany's war debts if they want to avoid another war.

Germany's huge debt would never be repaid, as Keynes argued, but another war would indeed occur, as he predicted.[2]

Nearly a century later, debt cancellation is still on the agenda, but it is the debt of another lost war, that waged against economic underdevelopment, for which the truce must be signed. It is estimated that by the end of the 1990s debts amounting to more than $150 billion had been accumulated by the world's poorest countries, on average the equivalent of 3 years of their income from exports. For a long time, creditor countries tried to maintain the fiction that this debt would be repaid. Nearly every month, meeting at what is called the Paris Club, the public creditors convened the finance ministers of the most indebted countries before a sort of tribunal, then asked them to wait in a room for their verdict, which sometimes took the whole night. The debt was continually adjusted in the hope of payment in better days. As happened in Germany after World War I, massive obligations can destabilize a debtor country that lives under the constant threat of bankruptcy but is unable to make payments to its creditors.

In theory, there is no better support for financial globalization than an aging population, today found in the wealthy countries, which invests in a young population, the emerging countries, to prepare for retirement. The final years of the twentieth century registered a spectacular increase in financial mobility—but at an immense cost. Studies have shown that 125 countries experienced serious banking crises between 1980 and 1990, while 70 countries on the path of development faced extreme financial crises, which entailed considerable social costs, consuming up to 10 percent of the affected countries' GDP.[3] Between 1979 and 1998, no less that 40 episodes of brutal financial reversals took place. Fourteen occurred between 1994 and 1998. When characterizing Latin America in the 1980s, the term used is "the lost decade." After a decade during which Latin American countries suffered the effects of the adjustment program, they finally benefited from debt reduction at the end of the 1980s under the Brady Plan. The cancellations affected 30 percent of Mexico's total debt, and nearly 80 percent in Bolivia's case. These reductions were followed by an immediate resumption of economic growth, which proved to be insufficient. The creditors' mistrust with respect to Brazil, for example, rendered its debt unsustainable, the compound effect of risk premia being by themselves sufficient to make it explode.

Criticisms of financial globalization are at the center of reproaches aimed at globalization at large. Begun in France, the ATTAC (Association for the Taxation of Financial Transactions) movement has built up a large constituency. It was behind the social forums of Porto Alegre, and it was active in demonstrations at meetings of the Group of Seven. ATTAC took up the economist James Tobin's suggestion to tax financial transactions so as to "throw some sand in the wheels of our excessively efficient international money markets."[4] A number of studies, including some published by the International Monetary Fund, showed that financial globalization was indeed a destabilizing factor, and that ultimately it would be wiser for poor countries to withdraw from it. Beyond the technical questions that it raises, the "Tobin tax" owes its popularity to the fact that it symbolically denounces the new power that international financial markets have over the functioning of economies while also shedding light on the need to aid the poorest countries. From a strictly technical point of view, however, the surest effect of instituting the "Tobin tax" would be to diminish the volume of transactions, but is this an element of market stabilization? It would reduce "high-frequency" transactions (the daily back-and-forth of interventions on the foreign exchange markets), but it would have no effect on "low-frequency" transactions made by those who invest their money for the long term. Yet it has not been proven that it is the former that cause the problem; a number of economists believe rather that it is the "low-frequency" operators who destabilize financial markets, as attested to by crises in real estate that are just as serious.

However, when measuring its "political" effect, one can only be surprised by the enthusiasm the "Tobin tax" incited in favor helping poor countries, a goal that normally is off the politicians' radar screens. In effect, public aid for development sees its share constantly regress; on average it remains at half of the UN-established objective of 0.7 percent of GDP. By choosing to militate for formulas (such as the "Tobin tax") that have symbolic value but are technically questionable and too complex to implement, anti-globalization movements excuse rich countries from responding "hic et nunc" to the reality of their efforts in favor of the Third World. The simplest way to help poor countries is to make each government accountable to its own constituency for the funds it devotes to reducing global inequalities.

Financial crises also had considerable effects on industrialized countries, culminating in the 1929 financial crisis and the Great Depression. Since World War II, however, while many financial and real estate crises continued to be recorded, we do not observe many systemic crises in the sense of chain bankruptcies, which reduces their effects on the entire economy. Since 1929, industrialized countries have set up public institutions that can dampen financial crises. For example, the United States created the Federal Deposit Insurance Corporation, which protects individual depositors from the risks of bank insolvency. Laws against over-indebtedness protect individuals; bankruptcy courts do the same for firms. Today debtors are protected by private rights against excessive sanctions. Yet sovereign nations still do not have a bankruptcy procedure at their disposal; once they have fallen into the debt trap, they remain prisoners, without recourse other than to the generosity of their creditors.

Jubilee 2000

The Jubilee 2000 movement generated a comparison between a biblical narrative regarding the status of the poor and the experience of poor countries today. In antiquity, a bad harvest obligated a farmer to take out a loan. If the next harvest was bad, he could lose his land. Facing more unpaid bills, he could end up losing his freedom. The debtor had to sell himself into slavery in order to pay his debts. Debt, when it leads to slavery, creates a flagrant disproportion between the cause and the effect. According to Thomas Aquinas, there is a difference between legal debt and moral debt. One might also remember Shakespeare's play *The Merchant of Venice*, in which Shylock wishes to enforce a contract that gives him the legal right to a pound of flesh.

A difficulty arises, however. If the creditor anticipates forgiving a debt, will he still make the loan? This dilemma is foreseen in the Bible:

Take care to not let yourself be surprised by this impure thought, and to not say in your heart, 'The seventh year, which is the year of the repayment, is close.' And to turn your eyes away from your brother who is poor, without giving him what he asks of you, for fear that he will cry against you to the lord, and that sin will be imputed to you. (Deuteronomy XV)

Is it also necessary to count on the lender's moral sense? The most indebted countries fear that the risk of a future debt cancellation will deprive them today of access to financial markets. Is the contradiction fatal?

An analogy will illustrate what is at stake. Consider an alcoholic who wants to stop drinking tomorrow. Here is the trap he is in: "I will stop drinking tomorrow" implies "and thus I will drink today." Why deprive oneself of a last glass if one is sure to stop tomorrow? But the paradox is more serious. If he thinks "In fact, tomorrow I will not manage to stop," the conclusion is the same, inasmuch as drinking today also means that one will drink tomorrow. He thinks that the actions of who he will be tomorrow belong to someone else. The "I" that stops or continues to drink tomorrow is another "I" than the person today. In order to escape the trap and stop drinking, he must reconcile these two beings and say to himself "The man I will be tomorrow is the man I am today. If I want to stop drinking, I must stop today."

In a similar manner, someone who goes into debt pawns someone other than himself: the person he will be tomorrow, the slave whose fate he would like to ignore. He loses his integrity, by necessity or by improvidence. This is the reason why, in the Bible, the Jubilee cancels debt contracts without any contradiction. According to the Bible, the man who falls into debt pawns a being of whom he is not master because he belongs to God. Herein lies the second sense of *The Merchant of Venice*. Antonio pawns a pound of his flesh to help his friend Bassanio get married. Is the guilty party Shylock, or the Venetian merchant who usurps his human condition by pawning it?

The same questions arise concerning indebted poor countries. Debt is the favorite weapon of harried governments, which do not worry about letting their successors solve these problems. But who is identified as the one who incurred the debt: the government, or the people? Debt is a trap in the sense that it exempts governments that borrow from asking who will repay. It is like a drug that postpones to the next day the problems that it provoked. Debt cancellation, therefore, does not aggravate the problem. It resolves it. It obliges lenders to ask themselves the question that will come at the time of repayment. To demand debt cancellation when the country is obviously too poor to repay it obliges both lenders and borrowers to anticipate the integrity of poor countries.

The Group of Seven's summits in Cologne (1999) and Gleanagles (2005) finally decided to cancel most of the debt of the world's poorest countries. For the first time in their existence, the International Monetary Fund and the World Bank canceled poor countries' debts to them. Like the question of withholding life-saving drugs by appealing to intellectual property, the fight for debt cancellation uncovered a contradiction between legal rights and moral rights, which turned to the advantage of latter. In both cases, public opinion managed to attain by persuasion what a representative democracy would have achieved more directly through elections.

Governing without Government

The examples of medicine and debt show how strongly public opinion can influence the world order. Financiers and pharmaceutical firms push the reasoning to an extreme: What will happen in a world where borrowers never repay their debts, or patients never pay for their medicines? These two questions misrepresent the problem. Poor countries already do not pay for their medicines—they are too poor to buy them in the first place. Neither do they repay their debts—the amounts are excessive. In framing the battle around these two principles, bankers and pharmaceutical laboratories nevertheless reveal the nature of the question. It is not about debating economic stakes; it is a question of general principle. Building a viable international economic order requires having the legitimate means to make fair exceptions to the general rules. How do we make it possible for poor countries to have access to medicines without having to completely remake general procedures in the pharmaceutical industry? Who can be the legitimate guarantor of this process?

This role seems to fall to the large international agencies such as the World Health Organization (in cases of medicine) and the International Monetary Fund (in cases of debt). However, the World Health Organization, the International Monetary Fund, the World Trade Organization, and the World Bank seem to be driven by an agenda that escapes all control. They resemble government departments left to themselves. The World Trade Organization is charged with applying the rules of global trade as accepted by the signatory countries of the Uruguay Round. This organization never integrated essential aspects such as public health or the environment into its mission. As for the International Monetary Fund, it is the guardian (as much as it can be) of international financial stability, but it only barely or marginally tries to correct for the brutal effects of exchange-rate crises on unemployment and poverty in affected countries. Each of these agencies bears witness to a democratic malady that can be expressed as an inverse relationship existing between the legitimacy of these agencies and their scope of operation. The World Health Organization is entirely legitimate when it treats sanitary problems; it would lose this authority if it was asked to take on problems of economic inequality or development. The International Monetary Fund legitimately enforces bankruptcy procedures for countries that are overly indebted, but it would lose its legitimacy if it were asked to intervene in questions of public health.

In fact, there are two problems at hand. The first is that there remain great worldwide public goods that are still not covered by an agency worthy of the name. The environment is the first fundamental example that comes to mind. One cannot continue for long leaving to private regulation the question of global warming, the opening of the ozone layer, or the disappearance of species. In this respect it is not surprising that, in the political scale, ecologists have been the first to want to abolish national states in favor of a single world government, to embody, in their eyes, the interests of the planet. The second problem is that, even when an existing agency is responsible for a certain public good, agencies defined by a "moral" compass, such as the World Health Organization and the Internal Labor Organization, have little authority. How do you ensure that child labor standards established by the Internal Labor Organization are applied to production norms and procedures, or that the World Health Organization's health guidelines are enforced? For example, today there is nothing in the concrete operation of the International Monetary Fund or the World Trade Organization to compel these organizations to observe the rules established by the Internal Labor Organization or the World Health Organization. A counterexample will illustrate what is at play. The Codex Alimentarius, a body of nutritional standards created by the World Health Organization and imposed upon the World Trade Organization, asserts that food deemed harmful by the World Health Organization should not be put into free circulation. Mobilizing public opinion will be necessary to change the course of these organizations' missions. How can passage from one body of principles to another be made (more) automatic?

A report by the French Council of Economic Analysis proposed an initial solution that could be implemented quickly.[5] It would require the World Trade Organization to demand an opinion from relevant agencies each time a trade dispute crops up regarding, say, a problem involving health or environment questions. The World Trade Organization would not be obliged to follow the advice, but it would have to explain why it was not following it. When this is done, the public can be exposed to the dispute and can then militate for revised trade agreements. But a more ambitious horizon can be envisioned. Jacques Delors proposed to create a Council of Economic Security in the United Nations. This could be called upon each time a conflict of standards interferes between agencies dependent on the United Nations system. The council, made up of sages with globally recognized moral authority, would be charged with resolving the problem. This formula will disappoint those who dream of a global state as much as partisans clinging to the sole idea of national states. But except for abandoning the enunciation of public norms to the markets or to sole self-enforcement by nations, it is essential to arrange for a regulatory framework whose task would be to bring moral norms and economic norms into coherence. If the world's problem is that today global consciousness is ahead of political reality, as debates concerning medicines and debt have demonstrated, it cannot be deprived of a practical outlet for long.

Reform and Revolution

There is palpable tension between those who would like to reform existing institutions today and those who ridicule them in the name of a revolutionary ideal. Serge Latouche, a French ecologist who has long argued against technological progress, flogs "house reformists" who would like to distinguish "good" capitalism from "bad" capitalism.[6] "In the economy there are perverse effects," he argues, "which can certainly be limited but whose essential nature is impossible to change. Adding the adjective 'durable' or 'sustainable' will not change a whole lot." The term "durable development," Latouche adds, resembles "the array of good intentions of proponents of another globalization." It is, he adds, "annoying that the World Bank and even George W. Bush do not say anything else." One could respond that Otto von Bismarck invented social security so that the people would think that he cared more about their welfare than the revolutionaries did. However, Bismarck would not have done it without the revolutionary threat.

That the movement once called "anti-globalization" now calls itself "altermondialist" is a sign of its evolution. For example, the debates that ensued after the publication of Michael Hardt and Antonio Negri's book *Empire* clearly express the tension that is still at work. *Empire*, characterized in the *New York Times* as the new *Communist Manifesto*, appeared to some of its leftist critics to be a displaced eulogy for capitalism.[7] Hardt and Negri use the word "empire" to designate globalization in a larger sense. "Empire," says Negri in a later interview to *Le Monde*,[8] "represents progress in the same way that capitalism, according to Marx, constituted a progress with relation to social forms and previous modes of production. Once the Empire is solidly established, those who are opposed to domination by the world's elite in the name of equality, liberty, and democracy will without a doubt find ways to oppose it." Negri views the "imperialist" temptations of the Bush administration as a return to the outdated ways of the nineteenth century. The emergence of a "reformist imperial aristocracy" would bring about a mode of global government adapted to the current state of globalization. Such a (reformist?) attitude would enrage Daniel Bensaïd, a French philosopher and an influential member of the Revolutionary Communist League. "Decidedly," he writes, "at the end of their intellectual Stations of the Cross, Hardt and Negri again come back to good old economic determinism, good old illusions of progress, and good old alliances (with the Empire's progressive elites against the old temptations of an obsolete imperialism)."[9] Bensaïd concludes that globalization and its institutions are irredeemable in practice. This opposition proves how much remains open, even at the heart of the altermondialist movement, regarding the proper attitude to adopt toward globalization. The line between globalization and its enemies goes through this movement.

Also entirely characteristic of the misunderstanding of globalization is the manner in which the debate is engaged. "Through the decentralization of production and the consolidation of the world market, the international divisions and flows of labor and capital have fractured and multiplied," Hardt and Negri write, "so that it is no longer possible to demarcate large geographical zones as center and periphery, North and South."[10] The illusions of a world without borders can be recognized here, where the "death of distance" theory is unequivocally endorses. Bensaïd rightly denounces this illusion, but his arguments are as fragile as those of Hardt and Negri. "Today as yesterday," Bensaïd writes, "underdevelopment is not an aside or the expression of a delay with respect to advanced countries. It resides in the same condition of enlarged accumulation, just as specialization in India, colonial slavery, and opium usage were the necessary reverse of industrial capitalism's progress between 1860 and 1880." We can also see that this vision of unequal exchange, which makes poor countries the necessary countercondition of rich countries' wealth, was false. The drama of the current globalization has an exact opposite cause: the poverty of the poor is gratuitous and useless.

Global capitalism is not simply capitalism. This is the whole problem. The tragedy of the poorest countries is that they want to participate, without losing themselves, in a world that essentially ignores them. To make the world more just, it will be necessary to create institutions that facilitate poor countries' entrance into global capitalism while constructing mechanisms that open a public space outside the realm of economic forces. It is this partly contradictory task that awaits our generation.

Conclusion

Europe took control of the world in half a millennium. Standing on the shoulders of the great Eurasian civilizations, it destroyed pre-Colombian civilizations before enslaving the Chinese, Indian, and Muslim civilizations, from whom it previously appropriated major inventions. In 1913, Europe and its new settlements reigned over the world. Only Japan escaped this hegemony.

It is tempting to interpret today's globalization as the continuation by other means of the ongoing Westernization of the world. Whether the emphasis is placed on economic domination or on cultural domination, the West seems to be finishing the work it began 500 years ago. This reading of history equally drives the interpretation that rejects globalization.

Portraying globalization as a "clash of civilizations" or as a "world class struggle" has the merit of historical simplicity, but it confuses myth and reality. The principal problem with globalization today is not that it sharpens religious conflicts or class struggles; it is that *globalization does not keep its promises*. Globalization creates a strange world that nourishes the feeling of exploitation while in fact exploiting only a bit or not at all. It creates an image of new closeness between nations that is only virtual, not real.

Development, as analyzed by Amartya Sen, consists of giving peoples and societies the means to build destinies worthy of their expectations. The problem of globalization up to now is it has altered people's expectations more than it has increased their ability to act. Even in the *a priori* most favorable cases, the situation remains overwhelming. If China's eastern seaboard becomes the world's new factory, 800 million poor peasants will hope to obtain the right to go and live there. More than half of India's population still does not know how to read or write. Before the poor countries can become prosperous in their own right, considerable tasks remain for them. Half of the world's people live on less than $2 a day. Everything that will allow them to become fully vested participants in globalization remains to be done. The poor countries must build roads, educate their children, and master technologies that are constantly evolving. Access to the Internet requires telephone lines. In order to prescribe medicines, doctors are needed. For the majority of the poor inhabitants of our planet, globalization remains an inaccessible idea.

For a long time it was thought that global commerce was responsible for enlarging the gap between the rich and the poor during the nineteenth century, foreign trade having accelerated England's industrialization and curbed India's. This interpretation should be rather good news for poor countries, since today the opposite is occurring. However, India suffered from a much heavier handicap—one that also hindered many other poor countries after they gained independence. Indian development was imprisoned by a sometimes colonialist conception of capitalism more than by capitalism as such. Today it is believed that capitalism is not capable of producing the "spirit" that it needs to prosper. Max Weber imputed this impetus to Protestantism. Many others have seen it as a Western characteristic. But the spectacular economic divergence of Taiwan and mainland China after World War II illustrates the fragility of the latter thesis. That demographic and sociological similarities between an Islamic nation and a neighboring non-Islamic country are much stronger than those between two spatially separated Islamic countries leads to a similar conclusion: that role models are drawn from larger pools than nations or religions.

Samuel Huntington's observation that the Middle Eastern youths who hijack an American airliner may wear jeans and drink Coca-Cola can be read with another meaning: Though they hijack the American plane, they privately seek the American way of life. Iranians can burn an American flag before the television cameras and still adopt in private the behavior they denounce in public. Whoever saw the film *Ten* by the Iranian Abbas Kiarostami can no longer doubt that women in Iran ask the same questions as their Western counterparts.

However, wealthy countries, by the sole fact of their existence more than because they economically exploit or culturally stunt other peoples, pose an existential problem for other countries. That today they create technologies for the entire planet's use is at once immensely useful (they pay the cost of experimentation) and an expression of tyranny. Everything happens as if they uniformly prohibited the discovery of other possibilities. The existence of the telephone or television makes it impossible to think what could happen had they not been invented. Technology is much more than simple instruments. The paleontologist André Leroy-Gouran explained that, thanks to the use of tools, *Homo sapiens* progressed in a cumulative manner, rather than through the direct transmission of thoughts or ideas from one generation to another.

For countries in the South, and to a certain degree for European countries with respect to the United States, to be dispossessed from creating new knowledge and new technology is equated with exclusion from History. A person is not happy simply because he consumes a certain vegetable. The process that drives him to make one choice rather than another is just as heady as the choice itself. Poor countries want sewers and medicines. These wants do not conflict with a desire to participate in writing a global history that does not amount to mechanically imitating the most advanced countries.

Understanding globalization requires holding at equal distance the universalism of those for whom the stages of economical growth are fixed in advance and the relativism of those championing the clash of civilizations. Because the human species is indivisible, each people is challenged by the technical or moral discoveries made by others. But the world will never be "just" as long as people do not have the conviction that they all contribute to discovering and molding a shared human destiny.

Notes and Sources

Introduction

1. Paul Bairoch, *Mythes et Paradoxes de l'Histoire Economique* (La Découverte, 1994). Bairoch himself thought, "provocatively," that it was "good news" to the Third World (p. 72) that it did not take one country to exploit another one to get rich.

2. Germaine Tillion, *L'Algérie en 1957* (Minuit, 1957). See also Bernard Chantebout, *The Third World* (Armand Colin, 1989).

Chapter 1

1. Jared Diamond, *Guns, Germs, and Steel: The Fates of Human Societies* (Norton, 1996).

2. Ibid., p. 14.

3. Ibid., p. 15.

4. Ibid., p. 15.

5. To use a formula by Jean Baechler, *Esquisse d'une histoire universelle* (Fayard, 2002.)

6. Diamond, *Guns, Germs, and Steel*, p. 20.

7. Ibid., p. 21.

8. Ibid., pp. 252–253.

9. Only for five regions can independent invention of agriculture be proved: the Fertile Crescent of the Middle East, China, Meso-America, the Andes in South America, and the eastern United States. Four other regions—the Sahel, tropical Western Africa, Ethiopia, and New Guinea—"could" equally have been at the origin of agriculture.

10. The first African shepherds, thus, had an immense advantage over the hunter-gatherers, whom they quickly ousted.

11. In 1647 B.C., horses allowed a foreign people, the Hyksos, to conquer the Egyptians, who were then left destitute. The Hyksos imposed their rule on the Egyptian empire for five centuries before being brutally dethroned. Later still, saddles and spurs allowed the Huns to terrorize the Roman Empire and its successors.

12. Diamond, *Guns, Germs, and Steel*, p. 91.

13. Ibid., p. 408.

14. Ibid., p. 255.

15. Michael Kremer, "Population Growth and Technological Change: 1,000,000 BC to 1990," *Quarterly Journal of Economics* 108 (1993): 681–716. Kremer's article was not cited by Diamond, but Diamond's book didn't go unnoticed among economists. A review and a commentary can be found at http://econ161.berkeley.edu.

16. Claude Lévi-Strauss, *The Elementary Structures of Kinship* (Beacon, 1969).

Chapter 2

1. Kevin H. O'Rourke and Jeffrey G. Williamson, *Globalization and History: The Evolution of a Nineteenth-Century Atlantic Economy* (MIT Press, 1999).

2. John Maynard Keynes, *The Economic Consequences of the Peace* (Harcourt, Brace, and Howe, 1920), pp. 10–11.

3. At the beginning of the nineteenth century migration increased to 300,000 people per year, culminating at nearly a million per year by the beginning of the twentieth century. Nearly 30% of Finnish immigrants traveled with tickets pre-paid by their families who were already established at the new place. This was also the case for 50% of the Swedes and 40% of the Norwegians.

4. Not until 1840 did the flow of the new voluntary migration surpass coerced African migration (O'Rourke and Williamson, *Globalization and History*, p. 119).

5. Between 1870 and 1910, the price of land in Australia increased by 400%; in the United States it climbed by 250%. During the same period, the value of land decreased around 50% in France and England. For the two countries where it attained the most considerable proportions, Ireland and Sweden, migrations explain, for them alone, the evolution of the worker's wage. Irish salaries grew to 85% between 1870 and 1913, Swedish salaries by 250%. The judgments brought against the migratory movements at the time are echoed in contemporary debates. One feared that emigration deprived the source country of its best resources, resulting in a relentless economic retardation. Incapable of industrializing, notably because their interior markets were too small to benefit scale economies, these countries were condemned to a decline. See O'Rourke and Williamson, *Globalization and History*.

6. In 1913, according to Alan Taylor, half of Argentinean capital is held by foreign investors; this is also the case for 40% of Canadian capital, 20% of Australian capital, and 25% of US capital.

7. Toward the end of the century, 55–75% of the textiles consumed in India had been imported (Paul Bairoch, *Mythes et Paradoxes de l'Histoire Economique*, La Découverte, 1994).

8. Arghiri Emmanuel, *Unequal Exchange: A Study of the Imperialism of Trade* (Monthly Review Press, 1972), p. 269.

9. Ibid., pp. 124–125.

10. Ibid., p. 178. Charles Bettelheim (co-editor of the series Economy and Socialism, in which Emmanuel's *Unequal Exchange* was first published) attacks the thesis in the preface and in the epilogue. In his

preface he qualifies it as "petit-bourgeois," adding that this terminology has nothing "pejorative" about it. ("It aims," he says on p. 346, "to place in relation to each other an ideological notion and asocial position.") He specifies in the epilogue that the thesis smashes the foundation of proletarian internationalism and that it is insensitive to the epistemological break inaugurated by Marx that established "capitalism's fundamental contradiction on the level of class struggle, which places in opposition proletariat and bourgeoisie" (p. 352) and obviously not the North's proletariat versus the South's.

11. Emmanuel, *Unequal Exchange*, p. 119.

12. Ibid., p. 130.

13. Ibid., p. 125. The list given by Emmanuel to support his thesis is dazzling. He characterizes New Zealand and Australia as "primary" product exporters as much as Nigeria or Colombia: "The copper from Zambia or the Congo and the gold of South Africa are no more primary than coal, which was only yesterday one of the chief exports of Great Britain; sugar is about as much 'manufactured' as soap or margarine and certainly more 'manufactured' than Scotch whisky or the great wines of France; before they are exported, coffee, cocoa, and cotton (especially cotton) have to undergo a machine processing no less considerable, if not more so, than in the case of Swedish or Canadian timber; petroleum necessitates installations just as expensive as steel; bananas and spices are no more primary than meat or dairy products." "And yet," he concludes, "the prices of the former decline while those of the latter rise, and the only common characteristic in each case is that they are, respectively, the products of poor countries and the products of rich countries."

14. Bairoch, *Mythes et Paradoxes de l'Histoire Economique*.

15. During the nineteenth century and at the beginning of the twentieth century, on average only 17% of exports of wealthy countries were headed for colonized countries; since exports at the time amounted to only 8–9% of the GDP of wealthy countries, it remains that the exports going to poor countries absorbed only 1.3–1.7% of the total production volume of these countries, of which only 0.6–0.9% were for colonies. Figures corresponding to the United States are even lower: 0.5–0.9%

of the GDP headed for poor countries; higher for Europe: 1.4–1.8%, but the diagnosis is not fundamentally different. The true challenge to the idea that rich countries needed the Third World markets is that of England. 40% of British exports were going to the Third World; since exports represent a higher part, the figure for the United Kingdom for the volume of exports going to the South equals 4.6% of the GDP.

16. The dominant opinion, before the publication of this study, went in exactly the opposite direction. In effect, it was thought that the product manufacturers, benefiting from the contribution of new techniques, would see their prices fall with respect to the primary products, which benefited little if at all from new techniques. In 1942, the great historical economist Colin Clark foresaw an increase in the exchange rate by 90% in favor of primary products on the horizon of 1960. The "orthodox" economists' conclusion to this paradox was not very original. If the price of merchandise rose with respect to primary products, it's because the demand was stronger for the former than for the latter, which merited this biting response from Emmanuel: "If we accept this principle, we will be obligated to admit that nothing will impede the general level of wages in the United States from one day falling below those of India, if, for example, the elasticity of international demand, respectively for American cars and Indian cotton goods, is reversed to the detriment of the United States, and if this situation lasts long enough to produce these effects. All our experience, all our intuition, all our knowledge, statistical fact and simple good sense contradict such conjecture."

17. From 1880 to 1929, cotton went from $300 per ton to $570 per ton, while during the same period, American wheat went from $44 to $51.

18. The index went from 66 in 1876 to 175 in 1990.

19. Gregory Clark, "Why Isn't the Whole World Developed? Lessons from the Cotton Mills," *Journal of Economic History* 47 (1987), no. 1: 141–173.

20. This intelligence of capitalism certainly isn't original. In the first years of the nineteenth century, English workers were still paid subsistent wages. Paul Bairoch (*Victoires et Déboires*, Gallimard, 1997) writes: "The daily wage of a British urban laborer around 1780

represented the equivalent of six to seven kilograms of wheat. It is probable that elsewhere, in India or the Third World, the ratio corresponded to five to six kilograms. Around 1910, the English wage passed to the equivalent of 33 kilograms of wheat; whereas it probably stagnated in India."

21. Albert Memmi, *The Colonizer and the Colonized* (Orion, 1965). Acemoglu, Johnson and Robinson ("The Colonial Origins of Comparative Development," *American Economic Review* 91, 2001: 1369–1401) also offer an interesting insight on the economic consequences of Colonization, which emphasizes the lack of institutional legacy in colonized countries where the indigenous people has not been exterminated.

22. Memmi, *The Colonizer and the Colonized*, p. xxviii.

23. Ibid., p. 70.

Chapter 3

1. For the average of countries in the Organization for Economic Cooperation and Development, the increase in GDP went from 12.5% in 1960 to 20% in 2000.

2. In the postwar years, the Third World's part in Western Europe's exportations collapsed, passing from 28% in 1955 to 14% in 1972. The disproportion between the North and the South is striking: the exportations of wealthy countries to poor countries represented only 2% of their GDP. The exportations of poor countries to rich countries represented a percentage five times greater.

3. David Ricardo, *The Principles of Political Economy and Taxation* (Dent, 1969).

4. The two principal authors to have developed "new theories of international trade" are Elhanan Helpman and Paul Krugman. See their book *Market Structure and Foreign Trade* (MIT Press, 1985).

5. Jeffrey Frankel, "Globalization and the Economy," in *Governance in a Globalizing World*, ed. J. Nye and J. Donahue (Brookings Institution, 2002).

6. The intensity of global trade is impressive when referring to trade of only industrial products. Two thirds of their industrial production is exported in France and England, half to the United States. At the beginning of the century the corresponding figure was 23% in France, 13% in the United States. See Michael D. Bordo, Barry Eichengreen, and Douglas A. Irwin, Is Globalization Today Really Different than Globalization a Hundred Years Ago? (working paper 7195, National Bureau of Economic Research, 1999).

7. See Richard E. Baldwin and Philippe Martin, Two Waves of Globalization: Superficial Similarities, Fundamental Differences, working paper 6904, NBER, 1999.

8. The Organization for Economic Cooperation and Development has devoted itself to a quantitative exercise that illuminates the importance of this idea, by redefining the tasks performed in our economy in a grid that aims to determine if a profession mobilizes knowledge or not. It arrived at a grid where 50% of occupations would be concerned.

9. See Daniel Cohen and Michèle Debonneuil, *Nouvelle économie*, Rapport Conseil d'Analyse Economique, 2001.

10. J. Bradford DeLong and Michael Froomkin, Old Rules for the New Economy available at www.j-bradford-delong.net. See also Carl Shapiro and Hal R. Varian, *Information Rules: A Strategic Guide to the Network Economy* (Harvard Business School Press, 1999).

11. In the case of CDs that can be swapped between computers, the situation is *a priori* different. It is easy to copy the product and diffuse it, whereas in the case of video a second VCR is required, one must spend time recording, and one must start over for each copy. Thus, it can't be excluded that the disk *industry* undergoes the impact of technologies pushing toward a cost-free structure. Will music in general and the singer in particular suffer? And from the start the artists took home only a small part of the total receipts. These are, certainly, elevated due to important costs, but it is these costs themselves which the Internet would reduce considerably. The record companies argue that they serve as a filter and that they produce and promote the recordings. Indeed, no one would suggest that an ethereal meeting between an artist and the public could spontaneously come about without

mediators. Yet other vectors could fill this role. Reviews could possibly play better than in the past the role principally held today by promotional campaigns. Concerts might again be the medium by which artists would be paid.

12. When Sears, Roebuck, a pioneer of mail-order sales, first opened, it bankrupted hundreds of stores who lost their clients in a single blow. It is amusing that the first expected victim of the Internet today is the mail-order business, which itself, moreover, did not fulfill all the expectations placed upon it. After the initial euphoria, its interests quickly stabilized around 10% of total sales, which is certainly considerable, but leaves 90% of the market to traditional intermediaries. By virtue of comparison, online sales represent less than 1% of total sales. With respect to direct "business to consumers" commerce, the hopes of growth that it inspired remain very problematic with respect to profits. See Bruno Amable and Philippe Askénazy, "New Business Integration," in *The ICT Revolution*, ed. D. Cohen, P. Garibaldi, and S. Scarpetta (Oxford University Press, 2003).

13. John Sutton, *Sunk Cost and Market Structure* (MIT Press, 1991).

14. Fernand Braudel, *The Perspective of the World: Civilization and Capitalism, 15th–18th Century, Volume III* (Collins, 1984), p. 25.

15. Ibid., p. 280.

16. Ibid., p. 284.

17. Anthony Venables, *Geography and International Inequalities* (London School of Economics, 2001).

18. L.-A. Gérard Varret and M. Mougeot, *Aménagement du territoire* (Conseil d'Analyse Economique, 2001).

19. Edward E. Leamer and Michael Storper, The Economic Geography of the Internet Age, working paper 8450, NBER, 2001.

20. See Andrea Goldstein and David O'Connor, "Production Location and the Internet," in *The ICT Revolution*, ed. Cohen, Garibaldi, and Scarpetta.

21. These new methods of production were not created by the computer revolution; they resume, in part, methods experimented in the

1960s in Japan and what is associated with "Toyotism." Nevertheless, computer science allows for a radicalization of its usage and creates new applications in which the idea of "networking" is developed between complex production units, at the heart of and outward of the firm (the massive externalization of sub-contractors playing a considerable role). A study conducted by Philippe Askénazy shows that data processing is in fact only useful on the condition that this reorganization of labor is in place. Starting with individual data from American businesses, it establishes above all that the computerization of businesses, all things being equally, is without measurable effect on the business's productivity. In the businesses "reorganized" according to the "lean production" methods, his estimations show that computers augment the growth of total productivity by a factor of close to 1% per year on average, whereas it diminishes in the others. In other words, the computer is a useless and costly gadget for businesses who don't rethink their organizational methods and, on the contrary, a precious and valuable instrument for those who adopt it. See Philippe Askénazy, *La Croissance Moderne* (Economica, 2002).

22. The activity of multinational American firms perfectly illustrates the double process at work (Gordon H. Hanson, Raymond J. Mataloni Jr., and Matthew J. Slaughter, Expansion Strategies of U.S. Multinational Firms, working paper 8433, NBER, 2001). The American multinationals' global business amounts to $21 trillion. They employ 7 million people. They are the "big power" that causes concern. The activity of multinational firms is in the image of global commerce, of which they are the principal vector; 77% of sales realized by the American multinationals were headed, in 1998, for the OECD countries.

23. In 1925, the United States still saw 90% of their imports divided between two sectors: products destined for the agro-alimentary sector and raw materials destined for the industrial sector. The importation of semi-finished products for the automobile industry, for example, didn't exceed 0.02% of total imports. Its importation of equipment goods in general didn't surpass 0.4% of total imports. In 1995, the majority of American imports were intermediary products bought for industrial firms. For the Europeans (France, Germany, and the United Kingdom), more than half of intermediary products were imported.

This process designates a new "vertical specialization," which is substituted for the "horizontal specialization," of which the baguette and the rye bread were examples.

24. All industries combined, the part of re-exportation of the multinationals is stable at 34.5%. It increases, however, for manufacturing industries from 34% to 44%; it decreases, on the other hand, for services from 41% to 34.5%. There exists a light shift between the distribution of sales and employment: 65% of employees and 77% of the sales are in the OECD countries. Activity outside the OECD countries experienced a shakeup over the course of the last two decades. 15% in Latin America and 6% in Asia in 1982. Henceforth, play almost an equal game: 11% in Latin America and 10% in Asia, where the rate of growth was spectacular—sales were multiplied by 2.5 and employment by 2. While global employment of the multinationals increased by 25%, it doubled in Asia in the period 1989–1998. In China, the progression was 53% each year. Is it necessary to see in this Chinese or Asian increase a traditional modality of direct investment: is it like a market in growth, or is it about a decision inscribed above all in the process of vertical disintegration? Twenty percent of the multinationals' sales are in fact in commerce and distribution (as opposed to 15% in 1980). This figure alone demonstrates the importance of the single activity of brand and product commercialization. In the European OECD countries, everything shows that the activity of the multinationals stays traditional. The part of exportations realized by its subsidiaries has stayed stable over the course of the last 20 years: about a third of the production is re-exported to other (European) countries

25. The number is much smaller in India, a fact precisely due to customs tariffs that apparently remain discouraging.

Chapter 4

1. In the fifteenth century, Europe's population decreased from 380 million to 370 million.

2. Amartya Sen, *Development as Freedom* (Knopf, 1999), p. 109.

3. Paul Bairoch, *Economics and World History* (University of Chicago Press, 1993), p. 129.

4. See for example William Easterly, *The Elusive Quest for Growth* (MIT Press, 2001).

5. Paul Bairoch, *Le Tiers-monde dans l'impasse* (Gallimard, 1983).

6. Samuel P. Huntington, *The Clash of Civilizations and the Remaking of World Order* (Simon and Schuster, 1996).

7. *Completing the Fertility Transition* (United Nations Population Division, 2003).

8. In establishing a systemic link between medical progress/improvement in health, a reduction in infant mortality, and a demographic explosion, we have omitted one fundamental factor. Despite recorded improvements, poor countries are still much worse off in matters of health: infant mortality remains at abnormal levels. In the richest countries (the highest 25%), four babies die per 1,000 births. In poor nations, 200 die per 1,000 births. The illnesses that affect them, including tuberculosis, polio, diarrhea, hepatitis, and meningitis, are largely problems present since the nineteenth century. Vitamin A deficiency contributes to the death of 8 million children a year. When 20% of infants die before age 5, the families are not free from economic calculations. More children are born than are truly desired in order to protect against the risks of mortality. A moderate decline in the mortality rate can very well produce a rise in the population, despite an accompanying drop in the birth rate.

9. Pakistan also has an extremely high infant mortality rate, 340 children for every 100,000 births, twice as high as Egypt's. This corresponds to the theory outlined in the preceding note.

10. *Completing the Fertility Transition.*

11. The percentage of Japanese aged 30–34 years who are not married went from 7 in 1970 to 19.7 in 1995.

12. In *Le Capitalisme utopique* (Seuil, 1999), Pierre Rosanvallon showed that the idea of capitalism in the eighteenth century also seemed to precede its reality. Adam Smith's book *The Wealth of Nations* was

published in 1776, even though the author seems to have no awareness of the great inventions, such as the steam engine, which would go on to mould capitalism.

13. Max Weber, *The Protestant Ethic and the Spirit of Capitalism* (Scribner, 1958), p. 27.

14. This section revisits an article by the author that was published in *Le Monde* under the title "Is There an Islamic Economic Curse?" on November 6, 2001. It is reprinted in *Chroniques d'un Krach annoncé* (Editions de l'Aube, 2003).

15. See Michio Morishima, *Why Has Japan Succeeded?* (Cambridge University Press, 1984).

16. See William Breit and Barry T. Hirsch, eds., *Lives of the Laureates*, fourth edition (MIT Press, 2004), pp. 74–75.

17. Bernard Lewis, *What Went Wrong? The Clash between Islam and Modernity in the Middle East* (Harper Perennial, 2003).

18. Ibid., p. 6

19. Ibid., p. 7

20. Joel Mokyr, *The Lever of Riches* (Oxford University Press, 1990).

21. Lewis, *What Went Wrong?* p. 7

22. Ibid., p. 45.

23. Bairoch, *Victoires et Déboires*.

24. The Mongols lost power in 1368. The Ming Dynasty, the longest Chinese dynasty, governed until 1644. See Bairoch, *Victoires et Déboires*.

25. In 1858 the English obtained authorization to sail their gunboats in China's interior and the right to settle and European trade in the interior.

26. Joseph Needham devoted 14 volumes to this in his compendium *Science and Civilization in China*.

27. Angus Maddison, *The World Economy: A Millennium Perspective* (OECD, 2001).

Chapter 5

1. William Easterly, *The Elusive Quest for Growth* (MIT Press, 2001), p. 68.

2. Ibid., p. 267

3. Lant Pritchett and Deon Filmer, "What Educational Production Functions Really Show," *Economics of Education Review* 18 (year), no. 2: 223–239.

4. As Alice Amsden writes on p. 289 of *The Rise of "the Rest"* (Oxford University Press, 2001), the general philosophy that inspires these New Industrial Countries is much more like getting the job done rather than "getting the prices right."

5. There is, however, a broad spectrum. South Korea formed immense and very concentrated industrial groups, the famous *chaebols*. Taiwan had an attitude that could be judged much more liberal—it is more like the small and medium businesses made the country's success. Taiwan's industrial sector is about one-seventh as large as South Korea's.

6. See Maddison, *The World Economy*; Bairoch, *Victoires et Déboires*.

7. In 20 years, only 2,000 have been counted.

8. In 1995, trade was 36% of GDP in South Korea, 30% in Malaysia, and 39% in Thailand.

9. According to Amsden (*The Rise of "the Rest*," p. 42), "investments in modern technology were small because it was more lucrative for entrepreneurs to manipulate prices of raw cotton and handloomed cloth behind tariff barriers than to aspire to becoming internationally competitive in either cloth or yarn."

10. Between 1873 and 1913, the number of Japanese students in primary school went from 1.3 million to 6.5 million and the number in high school from 2,000 to 924,000. The number pursuing higher education went from 4,650 to 56,000.

11. "The map of developed regions and that of temperate zones match up almost perfectly." (Bairoch, *Economics and World History*). As

Jared Diamond emphasizes, throughout human history countries in the temperate zone have been late to prosper, invalidating the idea that the climate would be equally good or bad on a region's capacity to innovate. What is certain, on the other hand, is that without adaptation to tropical climates, the temperate regions' innovations are often useless. Besides, ransom of an older success, the density of Asian populations (three to four times greater than that of Europe) does not lend itself to European agricultural techniques for which the machines that were invented had been adapted to the culture of vast lands weakly populated.

12. Xavier Daumalin and Olivier Raveux, "Marseille (1831–1865): une Révolution industrielle entre Europe du Nord et Méditerranée," *Annales HSS.*

13. Ibid.

14. Jeffrey Sachs and Andrew Warner, "Economic Reform and the Process of Global Integration," *Brookings Papers on Economic Activity* no. 1 (1995): 1–118; Francisco Rodríguez and Dani Rodrik, "Trade Policy and Economic Growth: A Skeptic's Guide to the Cross-National Evidence," *NBER Macroeconomics Annual*, 2000: 261–325.

15. Jeffrey Frankel and David Romer, "Does Trade Cause Growth?" *American Economic Review* 89 (1999), no. 3: 379–399.

16. In their careful review of tests bearing out the idea that trade is a factor of growth, Rodríguez and Rodrik show that the variable that principally explains Sachs and Warner's result is the variable measuring the exchange rates on the black market. The interpretation of this variable, as suggested by Sachs and Warner, is that it represents a tax on trade, in the sense that exporters must (in general) sell their currency at the official rate, while the importer (to a lesser degree) must buy currency on the black market. Obviously many other macroeconomic policy variables exist that correlate with the black market, such as financial repression, inflation, debt crisis, which makes settling the question of knowing if there are trade barriers at play extremely difficult.

17. Dornbusch's comment on the Sachs-Warner paper appears on p. 106 of the same issue of the *Brookings Papers*. For Rodríguez and

Rodrik, international commerce plays a positive role on a country's institutions. An open society, according to them, is less vulnerable to nepotism, fraud, and corruption. Along the same lines, Robert E. Hall and Charles I. Jones ("Why Do Some Countries Produce So Much More Output Per Worker than Others? *Quarterly Journal of Economics* 114 (1999), no. 1: 83–116) propose to account for what the authors call "the social infrastructure" of a country. Openness, in the sense that Sachs and Warner measure it, is one of these components. The respect for "rule of the right" is another essential trait. The social infrastructure index this is based on accords the highest level to Switzerland and the United States, and the lowest to Zaire, Haiti, and Bangladesh. Between these extreme cases, Hall and Jones show that there is a near-perfect correlation between the level of economic development and the index as defined in this manner. The question of causality remains obviously difficult to answer.

18. Rodríguez and Rodrik, "Trade Policy and Economic Growth," p. 317.

19. When said correction of purchasing power is done, what comes back into consideration is the fact that it costs less to live in poor countries.

20. There were never so many people living on less than $1 a day, but as a percentage of the world's population the figures of misery are a little less disheartening. The portion of the global population in a situation of extreme poverty is undoubtedly lower today than it has ever been. In 1890, 80% of the world's population lived on the equivalent of $1 (in 1990 figures). In 1950, the part of the global population living on/at this vital minimum was nearly half of the world's population. Today it is one-fourth of the world's total. See François Bourguignon and Christian Morrisson, "Inequality among World Citizens: 1820–1992," *American Economic Review* 92 (2002), no. 4: 727–744.

21. "Why Isn't the Whole World Developed? Lessons from the Cotton Mills," *Journal of Economic History* 47 (1987), no. 1: 141–173.

22. Labor certainly represents only a small part of the total manufacturing costs in the Indian case (2% of the total), whereas it represents 20% of the total cost in the US.

23. Daniel Cohen and Marcelo Soto, *Why Are Poor Countries Poor?* (Centre for Economic Policy Research, 2002).

24. In Singapore, chewing gum came to be regulated in the same way as medicine.

25. Sen, *Development as Freedom*, p. 247.

26. Ibid., p. 53.

27. Ibid., p. 53.

28. Samuel Preston, "The Changing Relation between Mortality and Level of Economic Development," *Population Studies* 29 (1975), no. 2: 231–248.

29. Robert Lucas, "Making a Miracle," *Econometrica* 61 (1993), no. 2: 251–272; Roland Bénabou, "Inequality and Growth," *NBER Macroeconomics Annual* 11 (1996): 11–92.

Chapter 6

1. Paul M. Kennedy, *The Rise and Fall of the Great Powers: Economic Change and Military Conflict from 1500 to 2000* (Random House, 1987).

2. Gabriel Ardant, *Histoire de l'Impôt* (Fayard, 1971).

3. Cf. Pierre Bezbakh, "Diocletien et l'edit du maximum," *Le Monde*, April 29, 2003.

4. Mokyr, *The Lever of Riches*, pp. 20–30.

5. The works of Augustin Landier and Stefano Scarpetta have shown that the creation of enterprises in Europe suffered from the fact that the sizes of newly created European firms were stabilized at a significantly lower level than in the United States.

6. Élie Cohen and Jean-Hervé Lorenzi, *Politiques industrielles pour l'Europe* (Conseil d'Analyse Economique, 2000).

7. See also Robert Boyer and Michel Didier, "Innovations et croissance," Rapports du Conseil d'Analyse Economique no. 10: 11–132; Cohen and Debonneuil, *Nouvelle économie*.

8. Huntington, *The Clash of Civilizations and the Remaking of the World Order*, p. 303.

9. This section revisits an article published by the author in *Le Monde* on December 7, 2001 under the title "L'Europe, un géant sans tête." The article is reprinted in *Chroniques d'un Krach annoncé*.

10. Lluís Navarro, *A la Veille de l'Introduction Physique de l'Euro: Un Bilan Critique de Trois Années de Fonctionnement de l'UEM*, Problématiques no. 9, Groupement d'Études et de Recherches Notre Europe, 2001, p. 38.

11. Élie Cohen and Jean Pisani-Ferry, "Les paradoxes de l'Europe-puissance," *Esprit*, August-September 2002.

Chapter 7

1. The "open science" model is itself, however, threatened by the proliferation of intellectual property. Paul David gives an example: In 1984, the Reagan administration granted the monopoly to exploit satellite images of the earth to EUSAT (Earth Observation Satellite); the cost of images went from $450 to $4,500 each and academic research immediately stopped. Likewise, the example given by Jean Tirole, Claude Henry, Michel Trommetter, and Laurence Tubiana in *Propriété intellectuelle* (Conseil d'analyse économique, 2003) shows that "patents, and the traditional licenses attached to them, have a significantly negative effect on the clinical offering of genetic tests and have led many medical units to renounce the administration of these tests and even the research concerning them." If excessively strict intellectual-property law can be counterproductive to the ulterior development of knowledge, the absence of intellectual-property law obviously poses other problems. It can discourage research purely and simply, at least in the absence of adequate public financing. It can incite innovators to protect their fabrication secrets and thus further reduce the productive use of an idea for the community's benefit. There is an equilibrium to be found.

2. After World War I, Americans were reproached for not having erased France's war debts. After World War II, when, having learned

from history, they did this, they were reproached for their arrogance. See Philippe Roger, *L'ennemi américain* (Seuil, 2002).

3. Morris Goldstein, Carla A. Hills, and Peter G. Peterson, *Safeguarding Prosperity in a Global Financial System: The Future International Financial Architecture* (Institute for International Economics, Council on Foreign Relations, 1999).

4. James Tobin, "A Proposal for International Monetary Reform," *Eastern Economic Journal* 4 (1978), July–October: 153–159.

5. Pierre Jacquet, Jean Pisany-Ferry, and Laurence Tubiana, *Gouvernance Mondiale* (Conseil d'Analyse Economique, 2001).

6. Serge Latouche, "D'autres mondes sont possibles, pas une autre mondialisation," *Revue de MAUSS* 20 (2002), no. 2 : 77.

7. Michael Hardt and Antonio Negri, *Empire* (Harvard University Press, 2000).

8. Stephane Mandard, "Le mouvement ne va pas se limiter à la contestation," *Le Monde*, January 27, 2002.

9. Daniel Bensaïd, *Le nouvel internationalisme* (Textuel, 2003).

10. Hardt and Negri, *Empire*, p. 335.

Index